Thembalethu John Kumatana

Journey of My Footsteps

Driven, Motivated & Inspired

Wishing you inspiration and motivation as you read my story. Thank you for your support.

I'm eager to hear about your journey with my book. Email your review and feedback to

footstepsbookseries@gmail.com

facebook page:footsteps Book Series

Instagram:footstepsbooks

LinkIn:Footsteps Book Series

Copyright

Copyright 2024
Thembalethu John Kumatana

The right of Thembalethu John Kumatana to be identified as the author of they have asserted this work through the Copyright, Designs and Patents Act 1988.

All Rights Reserved

No reproduction, copy or transmission of this publication may be made without written permission.
No paragraph of this publication may be reproduced, copied or transmitted save with the written permission of the author or by the provisions
of the Copyright Act 1956 (as amended).

Any person who commits any unauthorised act about this publication may be liable to criminal prosecution and civil claims for damages.

First Published in 2024

Proofreading and Editing by Busy Bee Editing
(www.busybeeediting.co.za)

Table of Contents

Copyright 1
About the Author 4
Preface 6
Introduction 7
Family History 9
The Influence of My Grandparents in My Upbringing 12
Education History in South Africa 15
A Mother's Love 18
Growing Up in Elliot (Khowa) 26
Early Church Life: A Personal Journey of Faith 31
My Hobbies 38
Friendship 44
Senior Secondary Education 47
Community Leaders and Influential Members of the Community 57
Life in Cape Town from 2003 Onwards 60
Life at Fairview and the Influence of Charles Back in My Working Career 70
Fairview Senior Colleague's Support 73
My Workplace Mother 88
The Good Samaritan 97
The White Brother I Never Had 99
Marriage Life and Culture 102
My Responsibilities As the Firstborn Son in My Family 110
My Mother My Responsibility 118
Raising Our Two Beautiful Daughters 124
My Role As a Present Father to My Daughters 136

Preserving Cultural Traditions	139
Appreciation Phase	141
Dear Angela and Travis Jones,	144
Dear Charles Back	146
Dear Heila Brand	148
To my Wife and Kids	150
Acknowledging the Role of a Book Cover Designer	152

About the Author

Thembalethu Johan Kumatana was born in Maclear on September 16, 1982, to his father, Bonisile Kumatana, and his mother, Nombulelo Kumatana. He is married to Nolusindiso Portia Kumatana; they are blessed with two beautiful, intelligent girls, Luphiwe Angela Kumatana and Alulutho Alison Kumatana. His commitment to his family and the preservation of his cultural traditions is a testament to his character and values.

He attended public school in Maclear between 1989 and 1991 and Joels Hoek Farm School between 1992 and 1993. He then moved to Elliot, where he attended Lundi Primary School between 1994 and 1997 and Masikhuthale Secondary School between 1998 and 2002.

After Matriculating in 2002, he moved to Cape Town to further his education. He attended Boland College Campus in Paarl as a human resources part time student doing evening classes, going from work straight to class from 2007 to 2010. He worked at different workplaces, the most noticeable one being Fairview Wine Estate in Paarl, where he worked from 2007 to 2016. The support and influence of his colleagues and mentors at Fairview played a pivotal role in shaping his career and personal growth.

He started a human resources outsourcing company in 2016 with his business partner Estienne Venter and now finds himself the director of a human resources company with him.

In 2022, he enrolled at the Blackford Institute for Counsellors. The motivation for him to become a counsellor came from a deep-seated desire to help others navigate life's challenges, overcome obstacles, and achieve personal growth and healing. Counsellors are driven by a passion for supporting individuals in their journey towards self-discovery, empowerment, and mental well-being. He is motivated by the opportunity he has to make a positive impact on people's lives, providing a safe space for clients to explore their thoughts and emotions, gain clarity, and develop coping strategies. The fulfilment that comes from witnessing clients' progress, resilience, and transformation fuels counsellors' dedication to their profession, inspiring them to continue supporting and empowering others on their path to healing and self-improvement.

Follow his series of 'Footsteps' books as he takes the reader on a mindful trip down memory lane and shares parts of the past that were truly made to inspire.

Preface

As I sit down to pen the pages of my life story, I am reminded of moments, both joyous and challenging, that have created the story of my existence. Each chapter, marked by its trials and triumphs, has contributed to the person I am today. This book is a testament to the resilience, growth, and self-discovery that have defined my path, serving as a mirror to my soul and a beacon of hope for the future.

Introduction

Welcome to the introduction of this Journey of Footsteps book—a heartfelt testament to a life and a journey filled with profound experiences, lessons, and love. Within these pages, we have the privilege of venturing into the depths of an individual's existence, exploring the triumphs, challenges, and cherished moments that have shaped his unique story.

A legacy is not merely a collection of achievements or possessions; it goes far beyond that. It is the imprint we leave on the hearts and minds of those who come after us, a reflection of our values, beliefs, and the impact we have had on the world. It represents the essence of who we are, the memories we have created, and the lessons we have learnt along the way.

As we delve into the narrative, we are invited to reexamine our own lives, to reflect on the choices we have made, and to consider the enormously important aspects of our existence. Through Thembalethu's experiences, we find inspiration, guidance, and a renewed sense of purpose. This legacy book is a tribute to the richness of human experience, embracing the joys, the sorrows, the triumphs, and the setbacks that are woven into the tapestry of life. It serves as a reminder of the indomitable spirit of the human soul and the power of resilience, love, and compassion to overcome even the most daunting of challenges.

As we embark upon this journey together, let us embrace the opportunity to gain experience from the wisdom gained over the years, celebrate the beauty of shared moments, and honour the legacy that has been entrusted to us. May this book inspire us to cultivate our legacies, to make a positive impact on the lives of others, and to live each day with intention and authenticity.

You are invited to immerse yourselves in the rich tapestry of this living legacy and discover the transformative power it holds. May it ignite a spark within us all—a spark that will guide us in crafting our enduring narratives, leaving a legacy that will be cherished by generations to come.

Let the journey begin.

Family History

As previously mentioned, I was born in Maclear on the Farms on September 16, 1982. Growing up in Maclear during the latter years of Apartheid was quite an experience. Even though I was still young, I experienced the sensation of tear gas in my nostrils and my eyes.

During the late 1980s, as young people, we were not allowed to go to town due to the riots. I can vividly remember that our parents' home did not have a television. If we wanted to watch TV, we had to pay around ten cents to watch our favourite TV show for thirty minutes or contribute towards charging a battery-powered car that was used as a source of power.

When I began my early education, my parents lived on a small, old farm called Kwa-Bingwa in Maclear. To reach school, I, along with other children, relied heavily on our mothers to accompany us as we crossed a river from home to school and back. On rainy days, we were not allowed to attend school as the river would overflow, making it impossible to cross.

During the Easter holidays, my parents found a rental place in a location near the school, which provided us with easier access to education. During those years, I did not see my father often, as he worked in the mines and would only return during certain holidays.

At that time, there were two schools in the township. Those of us still in kindergarten, attended classes in our community churches. The police often patrolled the schools to maintain order. Our exposure to white people was limited, and whenever we encountered them, we would run away, as we were taught to keep our distance.

As mentioned earlier, I come from a family of four children, and I am the oldest. My early education progressed well with the help of my mother, a bright woman. She had aspired to become a nurse, and her mathematical skills were sharp.

Unfortunately, she could not fulfil her dreams due to her being raised by my grandmother on the farms. She often recounted stories of how the farm owner's wife had taken a liking to her and wanted her to receive an education. However, when the farm owner and his wife got divorced, the door to education closed for her.

My grandmother worked in the farmer's kitchen, which often required my mother's assistance on busy days, causing her to fall behind in her schoolwork. She even had to milk cows when her brothers were unavailable.

Due to the traditional African customs of the time, one morning, three elderly men arrived at her homestead.

She described them as unattractive in appearance. It turned out these men had come to ask for her hand in marriage. Thankfully, as she made coffee, she overheard their conversation with the elders about their intentions. Her brother helped her escape on a bicycle early in the morning to Umtata, where her older sister worked, and she did not return until she met my father.

The Influence of My Grandparents in My Upbringing

As I reflect on the Footsteps of my Journey, I realise that my upbringing was not like that of many of my peers. While most children have the loving presence of both sets of grandparents in their lives, I only had the privilege of knowing my maternal grandmother. Growing up, I never had the opportunity to meet my paternal grandparents, and it is a void that has shaped me in more ways than I can articulate. My journey began in a small town on a farm in Maclear, where my grandmother worked tirelessly to provide for her family. My mother's mother was a constant presence in my life. She was a warm and caring woman who always had a smile on her face and a hug waiting for me. I have fond memories of spending summers at her house, listening to her stories, and learning valuable life lessons from her.

On the other hand, my paternal grandparents remained a mystery to me. My father rarely spoke of them, and whenever I asked about them, the conversation would quickly change. It was as if they were a taboo subject in our household.

As a young child, I did not question this absence too much, but as I grew older, I became more curious about my roots and yearned to know more about where I came from. I remember the first time I asked my father about his parents. His face hardened, and he muttered something about a falling out many years ago. I could see the pain in his eyes, and I knew not to press the issue further.

As I grew older, I began to wonder about the grandparents I had never met – what they were like, what stories they had to tell, and what wisdom they could have passed down to me. I longed to hear their voices, to feel their embrace, and to connect with a part of my identity that felt as if it were missing.

As I navigated my teenage years and entered adulthood, I found myself grappling increasingly with this absence. I wanted to understand why my grandparents were not a part of my life and how their absence had impacted me in ways I did not fully comprehend. I realised that I carried a sense of longing and sadness within me, a yearning for a connection that could never be fulfilled.

Despite this void, I drew strength from the love and guidance of my maternal grandmother. She instilled in me values of kindness, resilience, and empathy that have shaped the person I am today. Her absence in my life may have left a void, but her presence filled it with love and wisdom that continues to guide me on my journey.

As I look back on the Footsteps of my Journey, I see the imprint of my grandparents – both known and unknown – on the person I have become. Their absence has taught me the importance of cherishing the relationships we have, of seeking forgiveness and reconciliation, and of embracing the complexities of family ties. While I may never have the chance to walk alongside my paternal grandparents, their legacy lives on in the stories I carry with me and the lessons I have learnt along the way.

My journey is a decoration made with the threads of love, loss, and resilience. The footsteps of those who came before me have left an indelible mark on my path, shaping me into the person I am today. As I continue to walk forward, I carry with me the memories of those who have guided me, even if their footsteps remain unseen.

Education History in South Africa

During Apartheid in 1980, the life of a black child was profoundly affected by racial segregation and discrimination. Black children experienced an inferior education system compared to their white counterparts, having to attend poorly funded schools with inadequate resources and overcrowded classrooms.

The curriculum for black students was designed to perpetuate racial inequalities and the idea of white supremacy. Black students were often taught skills that would only prepare them for menial jobs, thus perpetuating a cycle of poverty and limiting opportunities. Access to educational facilities and resources was severely limited for black children. Many schools in black communities lacked basic amenities like libraries, laboratories, and sports facilities.

The infrastructure was often dilapidated, making it difficult for students as they had to learn in a non-conducive environment. Furthermore, black children faced numerous challenges in accessing education, as they had to obtain permits or passes to travel to schools located in white areas, which were often far from their homes. This resulted in long commutes and limited time for studying and extracurricular activities, which severely disadvantaged equal development and advancement under Apartheid.

For many young South Africans, the realities of Apartheid were inescapable. The racial segregation and inequality that characterised the country affected every aspect of daily life, from education and employment to social interactions and access to public spaces. Children and teenagers were exposed to the stark realities of racial injustice and the harsh divisions that permeated society.

The impact of Apartheid was felt in schools, where students were subjected to discriminatory practices and limited educational opportunities based on their race. The experiences of growing up in a racially divided society left an indelible mark on the consciousness of young South Africans, shaping their perceptions of identity, belonging, and social justice. The transition from Apartheid to democracy in the early 1990s brought about a sense of both anticipation and uncertainty for young South Africans.

The release of Nelson Mandela from prison in 1990 and the subsequent negotiations for a new political dispensation signalled a historic turning point in the country's history. For many young people, the prospect of a democratic South Africa represented a newfound hope for a future free from the shackles of Apartheid.

This led up to the first democratic elections in 1994, which was a time of intense political mobilisation and civic engagement, as young South Africans eagerly participated in the democratic process and embraced the opportunity to shape the future of their country.

The post-Apartheid era brought about significant changes in the lives of young South Africans. The dismantling of Apartheid laws and the establishment of a non-racial, democratic society opened up new possibilities and freedoms for young people, offering them a chance to envision a future based on equality, justice, and reconciliation. The end of Apartheid also meant that young South Africans could then access educational opportunities, public spaces, and employment prospects without the constraints of racial discrimination.

A Mother's Love

A mother's relationship with her firstborn male child is complex and holds significant importance in many cultures worldwide, including Africa. This bond goes beyond biology and involves emotional, psychological, and social dimensions that profoundly impact both the mother and the child.

In African societies, the firstborn male child often holds a special place in the family; he is seen as the carrier of the family lineage and traditions. His birth is celebrated with great significance. The mother's love for her firstborn male child is instinctual, deeply rooted in the vulnerability of pregnancy and the strong emotional attachment she forms with her child. During the firstborn child's early years, the mother plays a pivotal role in nurturing, teaching, and providing for their needs. From breastfeeding to imparting essential life skills, the mother shapes the child's physical, intellectual, and emotional development. The bond between mother and child strengthens through daily interactions, affectionate gestures, and shared experiences.

As the firstborn male child matures, the mother's role evolves. My mother became my first teacher, passing down cultural values, traditions, and knowledge acquired over generations. She taught me how to navigate the complexities of my community, how to respect elders, and how to contribute positively to society. The relationship comes with lofty expectations and responsibilities, as the firstborn male often shoulders family traditions and legacy.

The intimate connection between a mother and her firstborn male child is characterised by unconditional love, sacrifice, and protection. The mother's love serves as a source of strength for the child, providing a foundation on which they can build their lives. It is crucial to recognise that the dynamics of the mother's relationship with her firstborn male child can vary significantly across different African countries, ethnic groups, and individual families. As society evolves and modernises, traditional roles and expectations may shift, influencing the nature of this relationship. While my education was progressing well, my mother found a job as a baker, and my father continued to work in the mines.

Everything was going smoothly until 1989, when I started getting sick. My mother still recalls the trauma she went through during that period. It began one Saturday as she prepared to go to town. Our morning routine usually involved having porridge before playtime, but on that Saturday, she prepared African salad (mealie-meal and milk) for us. We sat around the table in the two-bedroom house they were renting. She handed me the house keys, which I had around my neck when suddenly I kicked the table and passed out. As she recounted this scene, tears rolled down her cheeks, and she explained that she had no choice but to stop working. The sickness had started as early as 7:00 a.m., and it seemed as if I had stopped breathing, lying lifeless on the floor. This ordeal continued for an extended period. Eventually, at around 10:00 to 11:00 a.m., I began breathing again.

When I regained consciousness, I was ready to play as if nothing had happened. They questioned me about what had occurred, but I had no answers. All I wanted was to play. Unfortunately, the sickness persisted and became a recurring problem, affecting my education as I was no longer allowed to attend school during my sickness episodes, which occurred on Wednesdays and Saturdays. The other days of the week were problem-free for me.

When I completed Grade 5 and was about to enter Grade 6 in 1994, my parents relocated to Elliot. Unfortunately, I did not secure a spot in any school in Elliot, which was heart-wrenching as I was being separated from the only family I knew. I had to live on the farms with my grandmother and uncles from my mother's side. Everyone I knew who had lived with me went to Elliot, and I was left behind to attend a new school where I did not know anyone.

To the best of my recollection, on April 4, 1994, during the Easter Weekend, I went to visit my aunt in the location. My father had also visited the area but chose not to see me. On his way back to Johannesburg, where he worked in the mines and used the Vaal Maseru bus services, there was an accident between Elliot and Indwe. My aunts from my mother's side had kept this information from me, but by sheer luck, I stumbled upon a newspaper lying around with a photo of my father lying in a hospital bed. If my memory serves me correctly, the newspaper was either the Daily Dispatch or Imvo Zabantsundu. As I began to read the article, tears welled up in my eyes. I longed to be with my mother, but circumstances at the time did not allow me to reunite with her.

Throughout that entire period at my grandmother's place, my mind was consumed with thoughts about my mother, and I yearned to be by her side. Unfortunately, nobody cared enough to provide me with updates on my father's condition or how my mother and siblings were coping. It was as if I was deliberately being kept in the dark.

According to the newspaper, the bus involved in the accident was overloaded, with some passengers even standing in the bus's aisle. Fortunately, my father was one of the three survivors of that accident, while one of the survivors was a member of the Skade family in Elliot who ended up in a wheelchair.

My father was airlifted to Cecilia Makiwane Hospital in East London, where he underwent examination and remained under medical care for over six months. During his hospitalisation, my mother had to care for my siblings despite not having a job and relied solely on the kindness and contributions of family members. We had no relatives in Elliot at that time, and it became my responsibility to bring them food every other week. I would provide them with mealie meal from the farm, as well as milk and sour milk. This meant that on the days when I had to deliver food to them, I fell behind in my schoolwork, and as a result, I failed that year in school.

While I was staying with my grandmother, the farmer decided to evict her from the farm. In those years, you could not remain on a farm if the farmer did not employ you, and my uncles had decided to seek better opportunities in Port Elizabeth (Gqeberha).

The school I attended was approximately twenty kilometres from where we lived, and on Friday, I returned home to find no one there. My grandmother had relocated to the township in Maclear without informing me, leaving my belongings outside a roofless house.

Neighbours told me that my grandmother had instructed me to go and live with my father's siblings. I did not have the same close relationship with them as I had with my mother's family, but I had no other choice. Despite my hunger, I had to walk another five kilometres to reach them. When I arrived, I was welcomed with little enthusiasm, and I knew I was in for a challenging time. As I adjusted to my new normal life, health problems struck me again. I found solace in the silence of not having to engage with anyone.

Before long, we took our final exams, and the treatment I received during that time affected my ability to concentrate on my education. However, I was not too concerned as the time for me to reunite with my family was approaching. In December 1994, my mother came to fetch me, and I could not have been happier!

Upon arriving in Elliot, I had to adapt to a pristine environment, but it was easier with my family by my side. The house we lived in was a two-bedroom mud house made from soil using cow dung for cleanliness, a traditional and sustainable form of architecture that has been practised for centuries in various parts of Africa. This type of house, often referred to as a "mud house" or "earth house", is built using locally available materials and techniques that are well-suited to the climate and environment of the region, the cultural significance of such houses, and the use of cow dung for cleanliness.

In January 1995, we went to Lundi Primary School to enrol. Still, history seemed to want to repeat itself when we discovered that the school was not enrolling new students from outside Elliot as they prioritised children from nearby schools. Fortunately, I made it onto the waiting list, and in May 1995, I was called to start my education. It was a challenging year as I had to adjust to a different learning style and become accustomed to the teachers. At my previous school, we had white Afrikaans teachers, and Afrikaans was our first language. That year, I failed, but I persevered and improved in the following year.

I began playing soccer at an early age, participating in junior teams and local street soccer games until I became a part of a soccer team managed by Bra Pieter (may his soul rest in peace, as he passed away just before I authored this book).

While growing up, my mother worked at a clothing shop called Cash Cutters, and she was the sole breadwinner in our household. After spending some time in the hospital, my father was discharged from Cecilia Makiwane Hospital, but he could not walk or work. Having my father at home was not as straightforward as we had thought it would be, as he relied on crutches and spent most of his day in bed, still in the process of recovery. During this time, my mother provided for the family, and when she received her salary, she would hand it over to my father to manage the finances.

The respect my mother had for my father was truly remarkable. It was evident that my father felt the strain of not being able to provide for his family. My mother-maintained order and kept everyone content. In our household, we were raised with the belief that everyone could perform all the household duties, from doing dishes to mopping the floor; there were no designated tasks for girls or boys.

By 5:00 p.m., before my mom returned from work, we were expected to be playing inside the yard. Whoever was responsible for making supper ensured that it was prepared. Witnessing the hardships my family faced, I decided not to wear shoes to school during the summer to save money. Even though my mother was not pleased with this choice, I persisted. Christmas was a big event back then, and I chose school clothes for Christmas instead of casual attire.

Growing Up in Elliot (Khowa)

Growing up in a community that is dismantled by drugs and alcohol can present numerous challenges and obstacles that can impact every aspect of a young child's life. As a child growing up in Elliot, a community torn apart by the ravages of drugs and alcohol, I was no stranger to the harsh realities that surrounded me. The once vibrant streets that echoed with laughter and camaraderie now bore witness to a different kind of soundtrack - one filled with the cries of despair, the whispers of addiction, and the echoes of shattered dreams.

From an early age, I learnt to navigate the treacherous terrain of a community besieged by substance abuse, where the allure of drugs and alcohol cast a long shadow over the lives of its residents. The faces of those consumed by addiction became familiar to me, their struggles etched into the fabric of our neighbourhood like scars that refused to heal. I watched as families were torn apart, friendships dissolved, and futures extinguished by the grip of addiction that held our community in its vice-like embrace. The once bustling playgrounds now stood empty. The laughter of children was replaced by the silence of abandonment and neglect.

Growing up in Elliot meant learning to distinguish between the illusion of temporary escape offered by drugs and alcohol and the harsh reality of the consequences that followed. It meant witnessing the toll that addiction took on individuals, families, and the community and grappling with the profound sense of loss and helplessness that accompanied it.

Despite the darkness that enveloped our community, there were moments of resilience, hope, and courage that shone through like beacons in the night. I saw neighbours banding together to support one another, community organisations offering a lifeline of assistance and resources, and individuals rising above their circumstances to create a better future for themselves and those around them. Growing up in Elliot taught me the value of resilience, empathy, and determination in the face of adversity. It instilled in me a deep sense of compassion for those struggling with addiction, a commitment to breaking the cycle of substance abuse, and a belief in the transformative power of community support and solidarity.

As I look back on my childhood in Elliot, I am reminded of the strength and fortitude that can emerge from the crucible of hardship and adversity. While the scars of addiction may linger, they serve as a reminder of the resilience and courage that define not only our community but also the individuals who call it home.

Growing up in Elliot, in a community dismantled by drugs and alcohol was a journey marked by challenges, struggles, and heartache. Yet, it was also a journey of resilience, hope, and the enduring spirit of those who refused to be defined by their circumstances. During darkness, I found glimpses of light that illuminated the path towards a future built on healing, renewal, and unwavering belief. Growing up in a household where the love of God was the guiding force, under the nurturing care of a devoted mother, while simultaneously being surrounded by the pervasive influence of drugs and alcohol in the community, can present a complex and challenging upbringing.

As a child raised in the love of God by a mother whose unwavering faith and devotion shaped my moral compass and values, I was immersed in a world of compassion, empathy, and spiritual guidance. My mother's teachings instilled in me a deep sense of love, kindness, and forgiveness, grounding me in a solid foundation of faith that provided solace and strength in times of uncertainty and adversity. However, the idyllic sanctuary of our home stood in stark contrast to the harsh realities of the community outside our doorstep, where the insidious influence of drugs and alcohol cast a long shadow over the lives of its residents. The streets echoed with the whispers of addiction, the cries of despair, and the shattered dreams of those ensnared by the grip of substance abuse. Navigating the treacherous terrain of a community besieged by drugs and alcohol while holding fast to the teachings of love and compassion instilled by my mother was a delicate balancing act that required resilience, discernment, and unwavering faith. I witnessed firsthand the devastating impact of addiction on individuals, families, and the fabric of our community as lives were torn asunder and futures extinguished by the allure of temporary escape offered by drugs and alcohol.

In the face of this pervasive influence, my mother's steadfast faith and unwavering love served as a beacon of hope and guidance, offering a lifeline of support and strength during turmoil and chaos. Her prayers, her words of wisdom, and her example of grace and compassion inspired me to navigate the challenges and temptations of the outside world with courage, integrity, and a steadfast commitment to my values and beliefs. Growing up in a household steeped in the love of God, under the nurturing care of a mother whose faith was a source of light and guidance, provided me with a moral compass and a sense of purpose that anchored me in times of turbulence and uncertainty. It taught me the power of resilience, the importance of empathy, and the transformative nature of love and forgiveness in the face of adversity. As I reflect on my upbringing in the juxtaposition of the love of God and the influence of drugs and alcohol in the community, I am reminded of the profound impact that faith, love, and compassion can have in shaping one's character, values, and outlook on life. It is a testament to the resilience of the human spirit, the power of love to overcome darkness, and the enduring strength that comes from holding fast to one's beliefs and convictions in the face of adversity.

Growing up in the love of God by a mother surrounded by the influence of drugs and alcohol in the community was a journey marked by challenges, struggles, and conflicting influences. Yet, it was also a journey of resilience, faith, and the enduring power of love to transcend boundaries and shape one's identity and purpose. It is a testament to the transformative nature of faith, the redemptive power of love, and the unwavering strength that comes from holding fast to one's beliefs and values in the face of adversity.

Early Church Life: A Personal Journey of Faith

Early church life plays a significant role in shaping one's spiritual journey and connection to God. In my own experience, my introduction to church life began at an early age when my mother ensured that I attended Sunday school at St. John's Apostolic Faith Mission. As a child, I did not particularly enjoy going to church but looking back; I can see how those early experiences laid the foundation for my faith journey.

At St. John's Apostolic Faith Mission, I was a member of the juvenile group, which catered to individuals up to the age of eighteen. Sunday school provided me with a basic understanding of biblical teachings and stories, as well as a sense of community and belonging within the church. While I may not have fully appreciated it at the time, those Sunday school lessons planted seeds of faith that would later blossom in my life.

When I turned eighteen, I made a crucial decision that would shape my faith journey moving forward. At that age, I accepted Jesus as my Lord and Saviour, a pivotal moment that marked a personal commitment to my faith. In accordance with the traditions of St. John's Apostolic Faith Mission, I was baptised at the age of eighteen, as the church did not baptise individuals under that age. The act of baptism symbolised a spiritual rebirth and a public declaration of my faith in Jesus Christ. It was a profound experience that solidified my connection to the church and to God. Through baptism, I felt a sense of cleansing and renewal, as if I were being washed clean of my past sins and embarking on a new chapter in my spiritual journey.

Early church life, particularly my experiences at St. John's Apostolic Faith Mission, played a crucial role in shaping my faith and identity as a Christian. The teachings, community, and rituals of the church provided me with a solid foundation upon which I could build my relationship with God. In Sunday school, I learnt the stories of the Bible and the principles of Christianity, while the act of baptism marked a significant milestone in my personal journey of faith.

Looking back on my early church life, I am grateful for the guidance and support that I received from my church community. The lessons learnt and the experiences shared helped me navigate life's challenges and deepen my relationship with God. Early church life may have seemed routine and obligatory at times, but in retrospect, It laid the groundwork for a faith that continues to sustain and inspire me to this day.

Being a juvenile member of a church comes with its own set of challenges and responsibilities. There were days when I found myself torn between fulfilling my family duties and attending church services. I vividly remember waking up early in the morning to make tea for my parents, knowing that this act of kindness would lead me to skip church.

This decision often upset my mother, who valued our presence at church. However, I made it a point to ensure that food was ready for them upon their return to make amends for my absence. The conflicting emotions I experienced during those moments stemmed from a lack of enjoyment in attending church at an early age. While I understood the significance of religious practices and community involvement, I struggled to find personal fulfilment and connection within those church walls. This internal conflict manifested in my actions of skipping church and engaging in solitary activities like counting cars on the main road.

Counting cars became a form of escapism for me, a way to distract myself from the discomfort of not enjoying church and the guilt of disappointing my mother. It provided a temporary respite from the pressures and expectations placed upon me as a young church member.

However, as the hours passed, I would inevitably feel a sense of emptiness and hunger that could not be satiated by idle distractions. This cycle of avoidance and temporary relief only served to deepen my feelings of disconnection and dissatisfaction. Looking back on those days, I recognise the importance of addressing and processing my emotions, even when they are uncomfortable or conflicting. It was essential for me to acknowledge my lack of enjoyment in attending church and explore the reasons behind it. By understanding my feelings and motivations, I could begin to navigate a path towards personal growth and self-discovery.

While a sense of discomfort and disconnection may have driven my actions, they also served as a catalyst for introspection and self-awareness. Through this experience, I learnt the importance of honesty and authenticity in honouring my emotions and seeking fulfilment in my spiritual journey. By acknowledging my feelings and taking steps towards finding joy and meaning in my faith, I could cultivate a deeper sense of purpose and connection within the church community.

My days of conflicting emotions and actions as a young church member were instrumental in shaping my understanding of self-discovery and personal growth. By confronting my lack of enjoyment and addressing the underlying reasons for my actions, I embarked on a journey towards finding fulfilment and connection within my faith. Through introspection and authenticity, I strove to navigate the complexities of being a juvenile member of the church with honesty and compassion towards myself and others.

In the year 2000, a significant milestone marked my spiritual journey as I, along with my fellow brethren Vusumzi, was baptised. This pivotal moment not only symbolised a personal commitment to my faith but also marked the beginning of a transformative period in my church life.

For the next two years, I had the privilege of experiencing a vibrant and fulfilling church life guided by the late Rev. Mnyanma, who played a crucial role in shaping and moulding us as young believers.

The late Rev. Mnyanma was not just a spiritual leader but a mentor and father figure to us. His guidance and teachings went beyond the pulpit, as he took a personal interest in our growth and development as individuals and as Christians.

One of the key lessons he imparted to us was the importance of humility and modesty in our faith journey. Through his example and teachings, he instilled in us the values of compassion, service, and humility, traits that would become foundational in our lives.

Under the mentorship of Rev. Mnyanma, my church life flourished as I actively participated in various church activities and events. I found myself going to places I had never imagined, both physically and spiritually. Whether it was attending conferences, outreach programmes, or community service initiatives, each experience enriched my faith and deepened my connection to God and the church community. Rev. Mnyanma's mentorship was instrumental in shaping my understanding of what it meant to live out my faith in practical ways. His emphasis on humility and modesty served as a constant reminder to always approach life with a servant's heart and a spirit of gratitude.

Through his guidance, I learnt the importance of being grounded in my faith while also being open to growth and transformation. The two years spent under the mentorship of the late Rev. Mnyanma were transformative in many ways. Not only did I deepen my relationship with God and the church community, but I also grew personally and spiritually. The lessons learnt and the values instilled in me during that time continue to resonate with me to this day, shaping the way I approach life and interact with others. In reflecting on those formative years in church life, I am grateful for the mentorship and guidance provided by the late Rev. Mnyanma. His impact on my spiritual journey was profound, leaving an indelible mark on my faith and character. The lessons of humility, modesty, and service that he imparted have become guiding principles that continue to shape my beliefs and actions as a follower of Christ.

As I look back on those years of fantastic church life, I am reminded of the transformative power of mentorship and the profound influence that a spiritual father can have on one's faith journey. Rev. Mnyanma's legacy lives on in the lives of those he mentored, inspiring us to walk in humility, serve with compassion, and always seek to grow in our faith.

My Hobbies

From an early age, I was always drawn to sports. It was in the dusty streets of my neighbourhood that my love for soccer first blossomed, and it was in the grazing fields that I learnt to play cricket. These two hobbies became a significant part of my childhood and helped shape me into the person I am today.

Soccer was the first sport I ever played. I remember watching older boys kicking a ball around in the street, and I could not wait to join in. I was only around eleven years old at the time, but I quickly fell in love with the game. The thrill of scoring a goal, the adrenaline rush of running down the field, and the bond of teamwork all captivated me. I spent hours every day practising my dribbling, passing, and shooting skills, determined to become the best player I could be.

Playing soccer in the dusty streets of my neighbourhood was more than just a hobby – it was a way of life. The streets were our pitch, the walls our goals, and the cars parked alongside the side our spectators. We played for hours on end, lost in the moment, with nothing but the sound of our laughter and the thud of the ball against the pavement filling the air.

It was a place where friendships were forged, skills were honed, and memories were made. As I grew older, my passion for soccer only intensified. I joined a local youth team and began playing in organised leagues. The competition was fierce, but I thrived on the challenge. I pushed myself to be better, to train harder, and never to give up.

Soccer taught me the value of perseverance, discipline, and teamwork – lessons that have stayed with me to this day. While soccer was my first love, cricket soon followed. I was introduced to the sport by my teacher, who had been an enthusiastic cricket player in his youth. He taught me the rules, the techniques, and the strategies of the game, and I was immediately hooked. Cricket was a perfect blend of athleticism and strategy, requiring both physical skill and mental acuity. I loved the precision of bowling, the power of batting, and the strategy of fielding.

Playing cricket in the grazing fields near my home was a stark contrast to the hustle and bustle of the city streets. The fields were vast and open, with nothing but the sound of chirping birds and rustling trees to break the silence. I loved the feeling of grass under my feet, the smell of fresh air in my lungs, and the sense of freedom that came with being out in nature. It was a peaceful and serene place to play, a world away from the noise and chaos of the city.

Like soccer, cricket became more than just a hobby to me – it became a passion. I joined a local cricket club and began playing in unprofessional tournaments and matches using a tennis ball as our cricket ball. The thrill of hitting a six, the satisfaction of taking a wicket, and the camaraderie of a team victory were all experiences that fuelled my love for the game. Cricket taught me the importance of focus, patience, and strategy – qualities that have served me well in both sports and life.

Growing up, soccer and cricket were not just games to me – they were a way of life. They were a source of joy, a means of self-expression, and a path to personal growth. They taught me the value of hard work, dedication, and perseverance. They showed me the power of teamwork, sportsmanship, and discipline. In a world filled with distractions and uncertainties, sports became my anchor. They provided me with a sense of purpose, a feeling of achievement, and a community of like-minded individuals. They gave me a sense of identity, a sense of belonging, and a sense of pride.

Today, as I look back on those dusty streets and peaceful fields where my love for soccer and cricket first took root, I am grateful for the memories they have given me. They have shaped me into the person I am today – a person who values hard work, camaraderie, and the thrill of competition. As I continue my journey through life, I know that soccer and cricket will always hold a special place in my heart. They will always be more than just games to me – they will be a reminder of where I came from, who I am, and the values that have guided me along the way, and for that, I will always be grateful.

Cricket, often referred to as the gentleman's game, is a sport that has captured the hearts of millions of people around the world. It is a game that is not only about skill and athleticism but also about passion and determination. The sound of the ball hitting the bat, the cheers of the crowd, and the thrill of competition all come together to create an exhilarating and unforgettable experience for both players and fans alike.

My love for the game of cricket began at an early age, but it was not until I saw some of the greatest players in action that my passion for the sport truly intensified. One of those players was the late, great captain of the South African cricket team, Hansie Cronje. Cronje was not only a talented cricketer but also a charismatic leader who inspired his team to achieve greatness on the field. His ability to remain calm under pressure and lead by example made him a role model for countless aspiring cricketers, including myself.

Another player who played a significant role in fuelling my love for cricket was the legendary fielder Jonty Rhodes. Rhodes was known for his athleticism, agility, and fearless approach to fielding, and his acrobatic catches and run-outs are still remembered and revered by cricket fans around the world. Watching Rhodes in action made me realise the importance of commitment and dedication in achieving success in any endeavour, and his passion for the game inspired me to strive for excellence in everything I do.

Shaun Pollock, Jacques Kallis, and Lance Klusener were three other players who left an impression on me with their outstanding performances on the cricket field. Pollock was a masterful bowler who combined accuracy with pace to trouble even the most accomplished batters. Kallis was a prolific all-rounder who excelled in both batting and bowling. Klusener, on the other hand, was a hard-hitting batter and a dependable bowler who played a crucial role in many of South Africa's victories during his career.

As I watched these skilful players in action, I was struck by their skill, determination, and passion for the game. They embodied the spirit of cricket and set a standard of excellence that I aspired to emulate in my own cricketing journey. Their dedication to their craft, their ability to perform under pressure, and their love for the game served as a source of inspiration for me, driving me to work harder, push myself further, and never settle for anything less than my best.

Cricket is more than just a sport to me - it is a passion, a way of life, and a source of inspiration. The skilful players I have had the privilege of watching included Hansie Cronje, Jonty Rhodes, Shaun Pollock, Jacques Kallis, Lance Klusener, and Makhaya Ntini, who is considered one of the greatest fast bowlers of his time.

Born in a small village in South Africa, Ntini faced many challenges growing up, but his determination and talent led him to become a cricketing legend. These cricketers left an indelible mark on my heart and soul, shaping my love for the game and fuelling my desire to keep on following the game. Their legacy will continue to live on in the hearts and minds of cricket enthusiasts everywhere, reminding us of the power of sport to unite, inspire, and transcend all boundaries.

Friendship

Growing up in Elliot, my closest friend was Xolani Nteleza. Xolani and I would only see each other during school holidays as he stayed and studied in Johannesburg. As a city boy, he was exposed to the hustle and bustle of city life, while I was a rural area boy, accustomed to the tranquillity and simplicity of our small town. Despite our different upbringings, Xolani and I formed a strong bond that transcended our contrasting backgrounds. Every December school holiday, Xolani would bring in all the latest toys and gadgets that he had access to in the city. I was always fascinated by his stories of city life and the experiences he shared with me.

As we grew older, our friendship only grew stronger. Xolani became more than just a friend – he became like a brother to me. When I got married, he stood by my side as my best man, a testament to the deep connection we had formed over the years. One of the things that bonded us was our shared love for soccer and music. We would spend hours playing soccer in the dusty fields near our homes, cheering each other on and celebrating victories together. Music was another passion we both shared, and we would often spend evenings listening to our favourite songs and discussing the latest trends in the music industry. Xolani brought a unique perspective to my life, introducing me to new experiences and broadening my horizons. His city upbringing complemented my rural roots, creating a dynamic friendship that enriched both of our lives. Xolani Nteleza was not just a friend but a companion who walked alongside me through the various stages of life. Our shared interests in soccer and music brought us together, while our differences in upbringing only served to strengthen our bond.

Xolani will always hold a special place in my heart as a friend who shaped my childhood and accompanied me on the journey of growing up in Elliot. As I grew older, my admiration for city life continued to grow, and I found myself yearning to experience the vibrant energy and opportunities that Johannesburg had to offer. However, the reality of not having any relatives or connections in Johannesburg made the prospect of moving there seem daunting and out of reach. Despite this setback, I refused to give up on my dream of living in a bustling city, and I decided to explore other options.

Cape Town emerged as my last resort, and little did I know that it would turn out to be my own "city of gold." The moment I set foot in Cape Town, I was captivated by its beauty, diversity, and endless possibilities. The city's stunning landscapes, rich cultural heritage, and thriving arts scene immediately resonated with me, making me feel right at home. As I settled into life in Cape Town, I discovered a sense of belonging and fulfilment that I had never experienced before. The city's welcoming atmosphere and vibrant community embraced me with open arms, providing me with the opportunity to explore new horizons and pursue my dreams.

Cape Town became more than just a city to me – it became a place of growth, discovery, and endless potential. I found myself immersed in its dynamic culture, forging new friendships, and carving out a path for myself in this bustling metropolis. In hindsight, I realised that sometimes the unexpected twists and turns in life lead us to the most fulfilling destinations. While my initial dream of moving to Johannesburg may have seemed unattainable, the serendipitous journey that brought me to Cape Town opened up a world of possibilities and opportunities that I had never imagined. Cape Town became my city of gold, a place where dreams took flight and aspirations turned into reality. The city's beauty, diversity, and vibrant spirit captured my heart, transforming my perception of what a city could offer. As I continue to navigate life in Cape Town, I am grateful for the unexpected path that led me here and the endless opportunities that await me in this remarkable city.

Senior Secondary Education

In 1998, I started my higher grades education at Masikhuthatle Senior Secondary School in Elliot. Oh, this was fun because while we were still at primary school, we did not have a school of our own, so we had to take shifts in the high school. Our classes would commence from 12:30 to 05:00 p.m. When I got to secondary school, I could not go to school barefoot, and our School Headmaster, Mr Koti, was an extremely strict principal. He even checked if you were wearing socks or not. We would trick him and paper between the trousers and shoes or would wear one sock, knowing which side he approaches from. In the same year, 1998, my father had fully recovered and went to Cape Town in the Winelands and found employment with Simonsvlei Winery International, and life started shaping up.

During the year 2000, I met a pretty girl who lived on a street not far from my home. We would walk homeward together after school, as there were some boys who were troubling her from school. I had to protect her from them, not knowing I slowly started falling in love with her. As beautiful as she was, the thought of expressing my feelings to her and a fear of rejection kept me merely contemplating the idea. I finally decided to express my feelings, and we agreed to take it slowly as neither of us had ever been with any other person intimately. The rest was history.

My family's situation was not that bad, but I had taught myself to provide for myself at an early age as we had been taught everything from cooking to house cleaning to laundry up to the year 1999. I usually spent my June school holidays with my uncle Mzoxolo Matiwane. Oh boy, he was fond of me! I would visit every year. My uncle worked in Port Elizabeth (now known as Gqeberha). He worked on the farms as a dairy operator. The farm owner would offer us piece jobs to allow us to make some money. So, I would buy clothes for myself, and whatever was left, I would take to my mom; I was and still am very frugal with money.

The year 2002 was a year filled with unexpected challenges, losses and setbacks that tested our resilience and resolve to overcome adversity. I matriculated in 2002 which was a tough year as we faced lots of challenges during that year. We played a key role in motivating other students to pay their school fees and purchase windbreakers. Despite the challenging work we had put in, we were told that the matriculants would not have a farewell that year. This was a colossal blow to us, and we started having meetings with the School Governing Body (SGB). I have tried to remember who they were but without success. The matriculants of that year were incredibly young and naïve, and all we looked forward to was a matric farewell. Isn't this what any student who is doing matric looks forward to, and we were not ready to be told that we could not have it? For a child in Grade 12, the matric ball holds a special significance as it marks a significant milestone in their academic journey and symbolises the transition from adolescence to adulthood.

The matric ball, a much-anticipated event in the life of a child in Grade 12, represents a culmination of years of hard work, dedication, and growth as they prepare to bid farewell to their high school years and embark on a new chapter in their lives. It is more than just a formal dance or celebration; the matric ball holds a deep and profound meaning for these young individuals, serving as a rite of passage that marks their transition from childhood to adulthood.

For a child in Grade 12, the matric ball is a momentous occasion that embodies a sense of achievement, accomplishment, and pride in reaching the final year of their high school journey. It is a time to reflect on the challenges overcome, the lessons learnt, and the friendships forged along the way as they prepare to take their first steps into the wider world beyond the confines of the school gates. The matric ball is not just a social event but also a symbolic representation of the growth, maturity, and self-discovery that defines children's high school experience. It is a chance to celebrate their individuality, creativity, and unique talents as they dress up in elegant attire, walk the red carpet, and dance the night away in the company of their peers and teachers.

Beyond the glitz and glamour of the event, the matric ball holds a deeper significance for a child in Grade 12 as it signifies the closing of one chapter and the opening of another in their lives. It is a moment of reflection, gratitude, and anticipation for the future as they prepare to bid farewell to the familiar routines and routines of high school and embrace the challenges and opportunities that lie ahead.

The matric ball is also a time for young individuals to express their individuality, creativity, and personal style as they choose their outfits, hairstyles, and accessories to reflect their unique personalities and tastes. It is a chance to highlight their confidence, poise, and grace as they take centre stage and make memories that will last a lifetime.

Moreover, the matric ball serves as a platform for young individuals to strengthen their bonds with their peers, teachers, and mentors as they come together to celebrate their achievements and share in the joy of this momentous occasion. It is a time to express gratitude, appreciation, and love for those who have supported and guided them throughout their high school journey, shaping them into the individuals they have become. The matric ball holds a special place in the hearts of children in Grade 12. It represents not just a formal dance or celebration but a significant milestone in their academic and personal growth journey.

It is a time to celebrate achievements, forge lasting memories, and embrace the future with hope, optimism, and excitement. The matric ball is a symbol of transition, transformation, and new beginnings as young individuals prepare to step out into the world and make their mark on the future with confidence, determination, and a sense of purpose. In the true sense of a word, this is all that we asked for; it was our school's tradition to have this event for all the matric students. The question was, what made us different from the rest of the matriculants who came from the same school?

As we were negotiating and fighting for what we believed in, we heard an uproar. There was a group of parents who supported us in this quest. It turned out that in the later years, when I looked back, they were not just supporting us. They had their own agendas, and we were a perfect group of young people to pursue their motives. These were people whom we had regarded as parents and leaders, and for them to use us in that way was simply not on. Some of them had no children attending our school, and some SGB members had no children at our school, and they did not even care about our interests.

We were a young group of vulnerable students who had been manipulated by adults. An idea was planted that the principal and his staff were misusing the school funds. The allegations were unproven. Sadly, as a result, unwelcomed and uncalled-for behaviour erupted.

We were addressing a group of students in our assembly area when we heard that a group of students had held the teacher hostage in the staff room, demanding answers about the school's fund as it surfaced that the school's bank account had zero rands in it. There was a teacher who stayed on the school premises, and she had stopped paying her rent. Suddenly, we heard that there were police at the gate forcing their way in, and we felt that police had no business at the school, and a riot started. Stones were thrown at the police; chairs were flying and being thrown at our teachers. The learners had resorted to violence even though this had never been intended. The problem is that when you are in a group, you tend to take on the group's mentality. We tried to stabilise the situation. The teachers were taken to the police station for protection, and some students were detained for their behaviour.

Nothing was ever the same for Masikhuthale from then until the rebuilding was done in 2019. I took full responsibility for that as I was one of the students who were delegates in negotiating and holding meetings with school authorities. However, our intentions were pure. It was never our intention to cause the school to be vandalised. Later, we collected money together and attended a small celebration in the schoolyard without our teachers. This was one of the sad moments in my life, and I still ask myself what happened. Had it not been for that, what would all of us have become in life?

That occasion ruined a lot of careers, and some kids had carried the hopes of their families, and those events buried all that. Sometimes, you think you are doing something good, but you do not realise when you are out of line. I know that what happened in 2002 should never have happened. We tried to maintain peace and address our issues around a table. While we were in the meeting, other students started breaking things, and everything went out of control. The situation was uncontrollable. Vandalism is a senseless act that can have far-reaching consequences, not only for the physical environment where it happens but also for the individuals and communities affected by it.

The aftermath of vandalism serves as a stark reminder of the destructive impact of such actions, and valuable lessons can be gleaned from them. One of the primary lessons I learnt from that act of vandalism was the importance of respect for property and public spaces. Vandalism often involves the wilful destruction or defacement of property, disregarding the time, effort, and resources that went into creating and maintaining those spaces.

Acts of vandalism not only damage physical structures but also erode the sense of pride and ownership that individuals have in their surroundings. It underscores the need for people to have a collective responsibility to protect and preserve public spaces for the benefit of all. Furthermore, vandalism highlights the broader issue of social responsibility and the impact of individual actions on the community at large.

The repercussions of vandalism extend beyond the immediate damage caused, affecting one's sense of safety, security, and the well-being of people who live and work in the area. It serves as a wake-up call to the importance of fostering a culture of respect, empathy, and accountability within society, wherein everyone recognises their role in upholding the common good and contributing positively to the community.

Acts of vandalism serve as a sobering reminder of the destructive impact of thoughtless actions and the valuable lessons that can be learnt from them. It underscores the importance of maintaining respect, social responsibility, accountability, and community engagement in safeguarding public spaces and fostering a sense of unity and pride within society.

By reflecting on the lessons learnt from the acts of vandalism in 2002, individuals can work towards creating a more respectful, empathetic, and harmonious community where the values of preservation, collaboration, and mutual respect are upheld and celebrated. When a school is vandalised, several individuals and groups can suffer because of that destructive act. The primary victims of school vandalism are the students who attend the school. Vandalism can create an unsafe and unwelcoming environment for students, affecting their sense of security and well-being. It can also disrupt their learning experience, as damaged facilities and resources may impede their ability to engage in academic activities.

We wrote our final exams with an average of eleven per cent pass rate for that year, and the following years were disasters because of our behaviour. School vandalism has a significant impact on teachers and staff members who work at the school. They may feel demoralised and frustrated by the damage caused to the school property, which can affect their morale and job satisfaction. Additionally, teachers may need to spend time and resources addressing the aftermath of vandalism, thereby diverting their focus from their primary responsibilities of educating students.

Parents and families of students also suffer when a school is vandalised. They may feel concerned about the safety and well-being of their children who are attending a school that has been targeted by vandals. Parents also experience frustration and disappointment at the disruption caused to their children's education, and the negative impact on the school then impacts the community.

Community Leaders and Influential Members of the Community

In a society where community leaders and influencers hold significant sway over the thoughts, actions, and aspirations of young people, they must wield their influence responsibly and ethically. As pillars of guidance, inspiration, and mentorship, community leaders and influencers hold a position of trust and authority that can shape the beliefs, values, and behaviours of the young individuals who look up to them. With this influence comes a profound responsibility to act with integrity, transparency, and respect towards those under their care, ensuring that their actions are guided by a genuine desire to uplift, empower, and support rather than manipulate and exploit.

Now, on reflection, I realise that in 2002, we did not get the support we deserved from the community leaders and influencers. We wanted to hear them say how important the matric ball is for the future that lies ahead for the students. The relationship between community leaders or influencers and young people is built on a foundation of trust, respect, and mutual understanding. When leaders abuse this trust by manipulating young individuals to fulfil their desires, they not only betray the principles of ethical leadership but also jeopardise the well-being and prospects of those who place their faith in them. Manipulation, coercion, and exploitation have no place in the realm of mentorship, guidance, and leadership. When community leaders or influencers use their position of authority to further their agendas at the expense of the young people they are meant to serve, they undermine the very fabric of trust, respect, and integrity that should define their roles.

Young individuals are particularly vulnerable to manipulation, given their impressionable nature, desire for validation, and need for guidance and support. Community leaders and influencers must recognise the power dynamics at play in their relationships with young people and exercise their influence with care, empathy, and a genuine commitment to the well-being and growth of those they mentor.

True leadership is not about exerting control or influence for personal gain but about empowering, inspiring, and uplifting others to reach their full potential. Community leaders and influencers have a moral obligation to act as role models of integrity, honesty, and ethical conduct by demonstrating through their actions the values of respect, empathy, and compassion that they seek to instil in the young individuals under their guidance. The responsibility of community leaders and influencers towards young people is a sacred trust that must be upheld with the utmost care, diligence, and integrity. By refraining from manipulation and exploitation and instead fostering a culture of respect, empowerment, and support, leaders can create a nurturing and empowering environment that enables young individuals to flourish, grow, and thrive.

Let us strive to be beacons of ethical leadership, guiding lights of inspiration, and pillars of support for the young people who look to us for guidance and mentorship. By acting with integrity, empathy, and a genuine commitment to the well-being of those we serve, we can create a community where trust, respect, and empowerment form the bedrock of our relationships and interactions.

Life in Cape Town from 2003 Onwards

I arrived in Cape Town (Khayelitsha Site C) in 2003 at my uncle's place, my father's brother. My aunt and cousin lived in the house at the time, as my uncle had passed on long before. The household was different from what I was used to. People walked in and out; everyone did their thing, and no one worried about anyone else.

I soon got used to it, even though it was tough at first. I saw different scenes from what I had experienced before. Khayelitsha is a vast informal settlement with a mix of shacks with overcrowded conditions, which we had to live with.

We lived in a three-bedroom shack with about ten other people, so there was no privacy. We had no prior knowledge of what that was like. If you wanted the room, you had to scream until whoever was inside answered you. The houses here were very different from where I came from, and it took me a week to get used to sleeping between walls made of zinc. The stories I heard about these houses described how they caught fire like nobody's business. Life became increasingly uncomfortable as time went on. My cousin's brother, who worked in a Vodacom container, turned out to be one of the most feared thugs in the area.

One Friday morning, he approached me and asked if I had any cash as he wanted to go out partying with his friends. It turned out that I had R500.00 with me, which was part of the cash I would need for registration at Lagunya Finishing School. I eventually gave him the money, as he promised that I would have it back by Monday morning before I went to school.

On Monday, I went to his house, and he was not there. I ended up going to his workplace, in the Vodacom container, and he gave me his house key and instructed me on how to enter the house and to close the door once I was inside, lift the mattress and take the amount of money I needed from under the mattress.

When I lifted the mattress, I saw an enormous amount of money spread under the bed. I could not believe my eyes, and I took my R500.00 and an extra R50.00 as he had said that I should take any amount I wanted. When I handed him his house key, he asked me how much I had taken, and I told him my amount and R50.00, and he said to me that I was a fool and did not know about money.

I immediately left my uncle's house. One of my cousins had a shack that was not being used, and she needed someone to occupy it. I was the right person to do that. We went to view the shack, and we ended up sleeping there, with me sleeping on the couch and she sleeping on the bed. In the early hours of the morning, I heard a knock at the door. She answered, and the person outside introduced himself and walked in.

The guy who came in handed my cousin's sister a roll of cash and asked her to count it for him. While she was counting, I was sweating under the blankets because the man was speaking to her in an aggressive voice.

While my cousin's sister was counting the cash, the man said that it should amount to ten thousand rand, and my cousin's sister had only counted eight thousand rand.

The man started getting upset and said, "Are you stealing from me? I will shoot you now." I started sweating even more, and I coughed – A big mistake! He charged towards me, removed my blankets, and asked who I was.

She explained that I was her cousin from Elliot. She said that I had arrived last week. He came back to me, removed my blankets by force, and said, Who are you?"

I said, "I am Thembalethu (bra)", meaning Sir.

As soon as he heard that, he said, "I can see you are from the Eastern Cape. Go back to sleep." When he left, my cousin's sister apologised, and I knew I would not be staying there long.

During the day, as I was doing my laundry, the guy came back, and I was very scared of him. His name was Cala, and he said to me, "Come. I will buy you meat; your cousin's sister said I must buy you some groceries."

I knew there was no way out. I went willingly, but I was scared; we bought the meat, and I could only eat a few pieces, and said that I was full, although I was not really full.

He said, "I understand that you are uncomfortable because you are scared, and whatever is left, you can take home."

On our way home, he started recruiting me to become part of the gang by saying these words, "Here in Cape Town, there is lots of money to be made; you just need to meet the right people, and you will be rich." I knew that I was being recruited.

My mother's words kept on ringing in my head, and I knew if I did anything out of line, I would be defying my parents. I moved from Cape Town to Paarl, where my father worked and stayed at a winery called Simonsvlei, and my life started to make sense again. When I moved to Paarl, I aimed to save costs as my father had to support me and my mom and siblings at the same time. That meant that I had to walk ten kilometres to get to the train station. I would walk this distance in summer, and the heat in Paarl is amazing. It goes as high as thirty-six degrees, and in winter, the rains are always at around eighty to a hundred per cent. I walked this distance every day of the week as I did not have the taxi fare.

During school holidays, I worked as a casual in a winery. In South Africa, the minimum wage was R7.00 per hour. I worked during the December school holidays of 2004, and I remained employed until 2005. When my contract ended at Simonsvlei, I worked at a timber plant as a wood processor and packer. That was one of the most difficult jobs I had ever performed.

On some days, I did not even eat my lunch; I would go and lie under the trees, totally exhausted. I rolled logs from trucks and conveyors onto log decks, carriages and stacking bays, placed logs and wood billets onto conveyors and lathes for processing into chips, veneers and pulp, sorted and stacked timber during milling, placed timber in place for processing by machines and unloading cut timber from the tail end of machines.

I assisted with setting up and operating plant and ancillary equipment used in the manufacture of sheets and boards, transported processed wood products, such as plywood, chipboard sheets and panels, to work areas, cleared blockages in machines, assisted with measuring and cutting materials, packed and loaded finished products for transportation, and cleaned work areas, tools and equipment.

This type of physical work reminded me of my secondary school teacher, Mr Sigenu. He would say, "To live like a king, you must work like a slave,"

That quote never left my mind. As I was performing this hard labour, I thought of him. After a long day of work, I would get home, take a bath and go straight to bed. After a couple of months, I gave up, and I remembered the scripture about the prodigal son. My mom made sure that I attended Sunday school. Luke chapter 15: 11-32 states; ('How many of my father's hired servants have food to spare, and here I am starving to death') I said to myself, 'How many older men are out there who are supported by parents while I am busy killing myself with hard labour.' At that time, I was 21 years old. I resigned, and I went home and told my dad that I had resigned.

He said to me, "Son, you did not have to do that job. I could see what it was doing to you, but I did not want to stop you myself."

On Thursday afternoon, as we were having drinks with my friends, one of the guy's friends at the neighbouring farm mentioned that Fairview had a dispatch position and that I should go and submit my CV there. I stopped drinking immediately and went to prepare myself for a job seeking adventure. The gentleman's name was Nkosinathi Mbiba. He told me to be at the house as early as 07:00 a.m. on Friday, 27 October 2006. I was there as he had asked me to be. He took me to the HR manager at the time, Mr Cyril Ress (may his soul rest in peace). I had an interview and was informed that the job was mine if I wanted it. I could start on Monday, 30 October 2006, but I said I was ready to start now, and that was how my Fairview employment journey started.

When I went job seeking, I did not have lunch as you do not carry lunch while job seeking, as this could be interpreted as a bad omen. Coming from Elliot "Ekhowa," I was offered lunch by one of the most beautiful souls I have ever come across, Marglen Robain. She offered me a ciabatta and cheese, but there was something about it that I did not get; the Cheese smelled of goat's milk and it was white.

In my life or our household, we never came across white cheese. We only knew of the yellow cheese "Cheddar". I struggled to eat this food, but because of the people who gave it to me, I had to eat it, and the cheese had no taste, as my taste buds were not used to it. In the end, I finished my lunch and went back to work. That was a unique working environment where it was mostly quiet, but then suddenly, it became a full house. I worked as a dispatch employee packing wines and helping clients carry them to their cars in the hope that I would get a tip.

On Sunday, 29 October 2006, a group of tourists arrived at around 3:00 p.m. I saw a lady walking around, and I noticed that she was not doing wine tasting. I offered her a juice, and she accepted it. We started talking and as we were talking, she mentioned that she was from California in America. Our conversation continued, and she had one question or, rather, a comment for me. She said that I still looked young and asked me why I was working. Was it because it was school or college holidays? I answered her with honesty that I was working there, and that the day was my third day at work. I also explained my situation to her and said that I would love to go to college but that the circumstances do not allow me to.

I told her that my sister was doing Grade 12 that year, and my goal was to help her with her education as my parents could not afford to send all of us to college. This woman of grace's name was **Angela Jones**, and her husband is **Travis Jones**, and they have a son, **Carter Jones**. She then asked me for a pen and a piece of paper, and she wrote down her residential address and asked me to follow up on our conversation by sending her an email. We took photos together, and she went to join her husband in the wine tasting. This was the couple's first trip to Africa and South Africa, and I was there.

After work, I went home wearing my Fairview branded apron only to realise that I still had the piece of paper in my pocket. As I was having drinks with my friends, I told them how my day was and about the lady that I met in the tasting room, and their response was no, she was just playing you. Do you think people from America care about people in Africa? This was treated as a big joke when the day ended.

Monday 30 October 2006 was my off day at work and as I was doing my laundry in my pocket, I found the note again. I did my laundry, walked to the shop, bought myself a writing pad, and started writing a letter to her. I posted it on 1 November 2006.

I told my friends that I had decided to write to her and that I had already mailed the letter. They laughed at me until I got a reply in February 2007 informing me that she had spoken to her husband and that they had decided to sponsor my studies on one condition, which was that I would not quit my job. I started researching nearby colleges about part time college studies, and we found Paarl Boland College.

Because of my lack of understanding of the application process, I needed assistance with discovering what I was good at compared to what I had always wanted to be. I spoke to my father about this opportunity, and he spoke to one of his colleagues, Mrs Heila Brand, who did not waste any time before helping me with the process.

She arranged with the University of Stellenbosch to help me write a career aptitude test, which took me an hour. Growing up, I had wanted to be a counsellor, a therapist, and an attorney, but to help good people, the test results came out exactly right. My choice of subjects was either journalism or human resources management. I chose human resources management as I was already in a workplace, and I thought that could work perfectly.

Life at Fairview and the Influence of Charles Back in My Working Career

Charles Louis Back is the third-generation owner of South African wine and cheese producer Fairview, in Paarl in the Western Cape province. Fairview Estate is a third-generation family-owned farm located on the slopes of Paarl Mountain in the Winelands of the Western Cape.

The Fairview business is a well-recognised brand in South Africa and abroad and attracts more than a quarter of a million tourists each year. I started working at Fairview in 2007 in dispatch, pushing trolleys to customers' cars. I expected to do a job, make cash, and go home. But in January of the next year, I enrolled to study human resources management at Boland College.

One day, Charles Back (owner) found me in the garden where I was studying. During all that time, the owner of Fairview, who was the third-generation in his family to make wines on the farm, was in America on a marketing business trip as Fairview exports most of their wines.

Finally, with the help of Mrs Brand, I managed to enrol in Boland College, I informed the Jones family, and they were prepared to make payments. One day, I was preparing for my evening class and was lying in my stomach going through my books, and I heard a voice asking me what book I was reading. I was shocked because it was Charles Back the owner of the Winery. If I remember correctly, I was browsing through a personnel management textbook, and he asked me who I was as he had not seen me on the farm before. He formally introduced himself, and I did the same, and he wished me luck and left.

Two days later, he sent his accountant, Andrie Marais, to call me to the Goatshed the Farm Restaurant. He started explaining his admiration for what I was doing, saying that he was proud of me and of the opportunity that my employment had brought to me. and he mentioned that he would like to be in contact with the Jones family as he would like to share the responsibility of paying for my studies. I had started computer classes before I could type an email, and I sent the Joneses an email about my employer's request.

It all worked well, and Fairview and the Joneses jointly funded my studies. The collaboration of the Jones family and Fairview Wine Estate provided me with the opportunity to pay for my sister's university accommodation and stationery, and it also allowed me to send money to my mother. My sister was doing a bachelor's science degree in Industrial Psychology. I soon received a promotion to become a wine tasting host in one of South Africa's biggest wine farms, Fairview; I took the opportunity and worked in the cellar for one harvesting season.

Fairview Senior Colleague's Support

I have been fortunate enough to experience a workplace where relationships are not only welcomed but also nurtured, and the team of senior colleagues I found at Fairview were truly a perfect match that made my journey at the company much more manageable. From the moment I joined Fairview, I could feel the positive and welcoming energy that permeated the office. The senior colleagues who had been with the company for many years were quick to extend a helping hand and offer guidance and support.

It was evident that these individuals were not just focused on their own success but were genuinely interested in fostering a collaborative and supportive work environment for everyone.

One of the first things that struck me about my senior colleagues at Fairview was their willingness to share their knowledge and expertise. They took the time to mentor me, answering my questions, providing valuable feedback on my work, and offering insights that helped me navigate the intricacies of the company and the industry. Their willingness to invest in my professional development was truly invaluable, and it made me feel like I had a reliable support system to lean on as I navigated the challenges of my new role. In addition to their mentorship, my senior colleagues at Fairview also made a point of building strong relationships with me and the rest of the team. These relationships were not only enjoyable and fulfilling, but they also had a tangible impact on our work performance.

As we got to know each other better, communication flowed more smoothly, collaboration became more seamless, and our team became more cohesive and effective. The support and camaraderie that I experienced with my senior colleagues at Fairview did not just make my work more enjoyable - it also made me more successful. When I was faced with challenges or setbacks, I knew that I could turn to my colleagues for advice, encouragement, and perspective.

Their collective wisdom and experience provided me with new insights and ideas that helped me overcome obstacles and find creative solutions to complex problems. With their support behind me, I felt more confident in my abilities and more empowered to take on new challenges and opportunities. Furthermore, the positive relationships I built with my senior colleagues at Fairview extended beyond the office walls.

We would often meet for lunch or coffee outside of work, share personal stories, and celebrate each other's milestones and achievements. These connections helped us form a strong bond that transcended professional boundaries and enriched our work experience. It became clear to me that the relationships we had built were not just beneficial for our individual growth but also for the overall success of the team and the company.

As I reflect on my time at Fairview and the invaluable support I received from my senior colleagues, I am struck by how fortunate I was to have found such a perfect match of individuals who were placed on my path to help me through my journey. Their guidance, mentorship, and camaraderie not only helped me grow and succeed professionally, but they also made my work experience richer, more fulfilling, and more enjoyable. A workplace is a challenging environment to navigate. Still, with the right relationships and a supportive team of senior colleagues, it can become a place of growth, learning, and fulfilment.

The colleagues I found at Fairview were not just colleagues - they were mentors, friends, and confidants who made it easy for me to work with them and succeed. Their support and guidance have been instrumental in my professional development, and I am grateful for the opportunities I have had to learn from and collaborate with such exceptional individuals. Fairview truly was a perfect match for me, and I will always cherish the relationships I built there as I continue my journey in the corporate world.

During my time as a wine tasting host at Fairview, I had the privilege of working with the best-tasting hosts in the area. Heinnie Van Zyl and Enoch Zaleni were not only skilled professionals but also dedicated mentors who guided me through the intricacies of wine tasting and customer service. Van Zyl's passion for wine was contagious, and his extensive knowledge of different varietals and vintages was hugely impressive. He took the time to explain the nuances of each wine we sampled, helping me to develop a deeper appreciation for the art of wine tasting. Zaleni, on the other hand, was an expert at creating memorable experiences for our guests. His charming personality and impeccable service skills ensured that every visitor left with a smile on their face.

Both Van Zyl and Zaleni took me under their wing and shared their expertise with me. They taught me the importance of providing exceptional customer service and the value of creating meaningful connections with our guests. Their guidance and mentorship were invaluable to me as I honed my skills as a wine tasting host.

Working alongside Van Zyl and Zaleni was a transformative experience that helped shape me into the professional I am today. Their passion, knowledge, and dedication inspired me to strive for excellence in every aspect of my work. I am grateful for the opportunity to gain experience from the best in the industry, and I am proud to have had such incredible mentors by my side. My time working with Heinnie Van Zyl and Enoch Zaleni at Fairview was a truly enriching and rewarding experience. Their mentorship had a lasting impact on my career, and I will always be grateful for the lessons they taught me. As a young man from the Eastern Cape, my knowledge of wines was non-existent. The only alcohol I was familiar with was the traditional African beer that was commonly consumed in my community.

Wine tasting was a foreign concept to me, and I had never even considered the possibility of working in the wine industry. However, that all changed when I met Van Zyl and Zaleni. They were experienced wine connoisseurs who introduced me to the world of wines and taught me the art of wine tasting. They patiently guided me through the intricacies of different grape varieties, wine regions, and ageing processes. With their expert guidance, I learnt how to appreciate the subtle nuances of each wine and how to discern the quality of a vintage. One of the most memorable experiences I had with Van Zyl and Zaleni was during a wine tasting event where I made my biggest sale to date. A customer from the United Kingdom was visiting our winery, and I had the opportunity to highlight our premium wines to him.

After an hour of sampling various wines and engaging in informative discussions about each one, the customer was thoroughly impressed with our selection. He decided to purchase a large quantity of our finest wines, including several exclusive vintages that were only available in limited quantities. The total value of the sale, including shipping costs to the United Kingdom, amounted to R76,000.

This was a significant achievement for me, as it not only highlighted my sales skills but also demonstrated my growing expertise in the world of wines. The feeling of satisfaction and pride that I felt after making that sale was indescribable. It was a validation of all the hard work and dedication that I had put into learning about wines and honing my sales skills.

Van Zyl and Zaleni were instrumental in helping me achieve this milestone, and I am immensely grateful for their mentorship and guidance. After that momentous sale, my confidence in wine tasting and sales grew exponentially. I was no longer intimidated by the complexities of different wines and have now developed a keen eye for identifying exceptional vintages. I even started conducting my own wine tastings and sharing my knowledge with others who were new to the world of wines. My journey from a novice with no knowledge of wines to a confident wine enthusiast and salesperson has been a remarkable one. Thanks to the guidance and expertise of Van Zyl and Zaleni, I discovered a passion for wines that I never knew existed. Making that significant sale to the United Kingdom customer was a defining moment in my career, and it has inspired me to continue pursuing excellence in the wine industry.

As a young man from the Eastern Cape, I never imagined that I would find myself immersed in the world of wines and making significant sales to international customers. Still, with determination, hard work, and the guidance of mentors like Van Zyl and Zaleni, I have been able to carve out a rewarding career in the wine industry. As I was still getting used to the tasting host position, another opportunity came knocking at my door. This time, the farm payroll administrator had resigned, and this provided a perfect opportunity for me.

Charles Back came to me and said, "Young man, I have an opportunity for you to become junior wage clerk or payroll clerk." He asked me to take my time to think this through. I consider myself lucky because, at all times, or most of the time, I had the most influential people around me, people who wanted to see progress.

Marglen Robain came to me and said, "Bokkie, you will be stupid if you do not take this opportunity."

I said to Marglen, "Everything is happening too fast, and this worries me."

She said, "Go home and think and come back and talk to Charles." She said, "Charles does not just provide opportunities to people when he does not believe that they will succeed."

I went home, and I spoke to my father about this, and he said to me, "Everything that is happening to you is because you made it happen by being good to your mom and the rest of the family (son, take the opportunity)."

I went to work motivated to take the opportunity, and it went well. The departing payroll clerk gave me good training and was patient with me. 'Gloudina Botha, what a soul she is,' I thought.

I think the only thing that influenced me to take the position Charle's ability to work with people and the way he addressed situations. When Gloudina Botha left her role as my mentor, I was initially apprehensive about being left without her guidance in the world of finance. However, I soon found myself under the mentorship of a financial manager, Andrie Marals, who would prove to be an asset in my journey through payroll. Andrie not only guided me through the complex world of finance but also provided me with unwavering patience and support, for which I am grateful to this day.

I remember the first day that Gloudina announced her departure, leaving me feeling lost and unsure of how to navigate through the intricacies of payroll management. However, Andrie quickly stepped in to fill the void left by Gloudina, offering his expertise and support to help me navigate through the new chapter in my career. He patiently answered my endless questions and provided me with the guidance I needed to manage the payroll responsibilities successfully.

One of the things that truly stood out to me about Andrie was his patience. Despite my lack of experience in finance, he never showed frustration or impatience with my questions or mistakes. Instead, he took the time to explain concepts to me in a way that was easily understood and encouraged me to ask questions and seek clarification whenever I needed it. His patience gave me the confidence I needed to excel in my role and grow as a professional in the field of finance. in addition to his patience, Andrie also provided me with a great deal of support and guidance in my studies.

During our lunch breaks, he would take the time to review my coursework and provide me with valuable insights that helped me excel in my studies. His willingness to go beyond usual limits to help me succeed showed me that he was truly invested in my growth and development, both professionally and academically. Andries' mentorship not only helped me improve my understanding of payroll management but also allowed me to develop valuable skills that have served me well throughout my career. His guidance and support helped me gain the knowledge and confidence I needed to excel in my role and navigate through the challenges of the finance industry. I am profoundly grateful for his mentorship and the impact he has had on my professional growth.

As I look back on my time under Andries' mentorship, I am filled with gratitude for the patience and guidance he provided me. His unwavering support and willingness to invest in my development played a significant role in shaping me into the professional I am today.

The lessons I learnt from him continue to guide me in my career, and I am forever grateful for the impact he has had on my journey through the world of finance. Andries Marais has been an invaluable mentor to me, guiding me through the complexities of payroll management with patience and support. His mentorship has not only helped me excel in my role but has also provided me with the skills and confidence I needed to succeed in the finance industry. I am grateful for his unwavering support and the impact he has had on my professional growth.

Andries Marais will always hold a special place in my heart as a mentor who genuinely cared about my success and invested in my development. Human resources and payroll are two essential functions within any organisation. While HR focuses on managing employees and ensuring compliance with laws and regulations, payroll deals with the financial aspect of employee compensation. Both departments work hand in hand to ensure that employees are well taken care of, and that the organisation runs smoothly. In my role within the HR department, I quickly realised that I needed some mentoring when it came to labour relations matters. I understood the basics of labour laws and regulations, but I needed guidance on how to handle more complex situations and ensure that the organisation was following the correct protocols.

That was when Charles Back stepped in and made sure that I had the support I needed. Charles recognised that I needed some extra help in that area, so he arranged for me to be mentored by Andries Laker, a labour relations officer with years of experience in the field. Andries was appointed to guide me through various labour relations issues and provide me with the knowledge and tools I needed to handle these situations effectively. Andries took me under his wing and shared his expertise with me. He taught me about the different labour laws and regulations that govern the workplace, including how to handle grievances, disciplinary actions, and negotiations with unions. He also provided me with practical advice on how to communicate effectively with employees and ensure that their rights were being protected. One of the most valuable lessons Andries taught me was the importance of building strong relationships with employees and being a fair and consistent leader. He emphasised the need to treat employees with respect and dignity, even in demanding situations. He also stressed the importance of being transparent and honest in all dealings with employees, as this builds trust and fosters a positive work environment.

Andries also helped me navigate some challenging labour relations issues that arose during my time in HR. He provided me with guidance on how to handle difficult employee grievances, how to negotiate a collective bargaining agreement, and how to mediate disputes between employees. His mentorship was invaluable in helping me navigate these situations with confidence and professionalism. Through Andries' mentorship, I gained a deeper understanding of labour relations and how it intersects with HR and payroll functions. I learnt how to handle complex labour relations issues, communicate effectively with employees, and ensure that the organisation remained compliant with all relevant laws and regulations.

Overall, the mentorship I received from Andries Laker was instrumental in helping me grow and develop in my role within the HR department. His guidance and support allowed me to handle labour relations matters with confidence and professionalism, benefiting both the employees and the organisation. With the support of mentors like Andries Laker, HR professionals can navigate complex labour relations issues with ease and confidence, creating a positive and productive work environment for all employees.

Working at Fairview was not just a job for me. It was an experience that allowed me to enjoy my time there genuinely. While we had our fair share of work responsibilities, we also had the opportunity to participate in various activities that made our time there memorable. One of the activities that stood out to me was the indoor soccer and indoor cricket games that we would participate in during our breaks. It was a wonderful way to unwind and have some fun with my colleagues.

However, what I enjoyed the most was running sessions with the legend Donald Mouton. Donald Mouton is an experienced runner who had run numerous marathons and was known for his incredible speed and endurance. Running with him was both challenging and inspiring. I learnt a lot from him, and he pushed me to become a better runner.

One of the highlights of my time at Fairview was participating in the trail marathons, especially the famous Fairview Mountain Goat Run. This run was known for its challenging terrain and breathtaking views. The edition of the mountain goat run that I participated in was particularly memorable as I managed to make it into the top ten finishers. The race was intense and demanding, with steep inclines and rugged terrain, but the sense of accomplishment I felt when I crossed the finish line in the top ten made it all worth it. I had trained hard for the race, and it paid off.

Donald Mouton's guidance and encouragement played a significant role in my success. The atmosphere at Fairview during the mountain goat run was electric. There was a sense of camaraderie among the participants, all of whom shared a love for running and a passion for pushing themselves to their limits. Crossing that finish line felt like a victory, not just for me but for everyone else who had participated in the race.

Looking back now, I realise that my time at Fairview was more than just work. It was an opportunity to challenge myself, both physically and mentally, and to push myself beyond my limits. I am grateful for the experiences and memories that I gained during my time there, and I will always look back on my time at Fairview with fondness and pride.

I view my career path as a prime example of a meaningful empowerment venture: It started on merit, and the investment included a longer-term and purposeful transfer of skills and a chance to develop my own identity while receiving financial support. When it comes to black economic empowerment, businesses need to know that the person (beneficiary) is fully fit for the project and will survive, so there needs to be merit. However, in that process, it is also crucial that there is mentorship. I could not have asked for a better mentor than Charles.

One of the important lessons he takes forward in his own business is his exceptional conduct when working with people. It comes from the way Charles sees people. He views them not merely as employees working for Fairview. He values people. He sees everyone as colleagues. That has taught me that no matter the situation, there is a minimum standard for dealing with others; Absolutely!

My Workplace Mother

In every workplace, there always seems to be one special colleague who stands out as a mother figure to everyone. In my case, that person was Trudie Brand. Trudie was not only a co-worker, but she was also a mentor, a friend, and a confidante. She had a way of making everyone feel comfortable and cared for, and she always knew exactly what to say or do when the going got tough.

I remember the first time I met Trudie. It was my first day at the office, and I was feeling overwhelmed and nervous. As I stumbled through the introductions, trying to find my way around, Trudie approached me with a warm smile and a welcoming demeanour. From that moment on, I knew that she was someone special.

As time passed, I found myself turning to Trudie increasingly for guidance and support. Whenever I had a problem at work or even in my personal life, Trudie was always there to listen and offer advice. She had a way of calming my fears and doubts, and she always knew exactly what to say to make me feel better.

One of the things that I appreciated most about Trudie was her ability to empathise with others. She had a knack for sensing when someone was struggling, and she would always take the time to reach out and offer a helping hand. Whether it was a kind word of encouragement or a thoughtful gesture, Trudie always went out of her way to make sure that everyone around her felt supported and valued. There were many times when the pressures of work seemed overwhelming, and I found myself on the verge of tears. In those moments, I would seek out Trudie, knowing that she would be there to comfort me and lend a listening ear. She always had a way of making me feel heard and understood, and she never judged me on my vulnerabilities or insecurities.

Trudie was not just a mother figure to me but to everyone in the office. She had a natural ability to nurture and care for those around her, and she took on the role of mentor and adviser with grace and compassion. She was a true leader in every sense of the word, and her presence in the workplace was a source of comfort and inspiration for all of us.

In addition to her caring nature, Trudie also had a strong work ethic and a sense of professionalism that set her apart from others. She was dedicated to her job and always went beyond limits to ensure that things were done right. Her diligence and commitment to excellence were evident in everything she did, and her colleagues admired and respected her for her hard work and diligence. Despite her busy schedule and demanding responsibilities, Trudie always found time to lend a helping hand to those in need. Whether it was staying late to assist with a project or offering a word of encouragement to a struggling colleague, Trudie never hesitated to go the extra mile. Her selflessness and generosity were qualities that endeared her to everyone she encountered, and she was truly a shining example of what it means to be a supportive and caring colleague.

As I reflect on my time working with Trudie, I am filled with gratitude for the impact she had on my life. She was more than just a co-worker; she was a mentor, a friend, and a source of strength and encouragement. Her wisdom and guidance helped me navigate the challenges of the workplace, and her kindness and compassion made each day a little brighter. Trudie Brand was a special colleague who touched the lives of everyone around her. Her nurturing spirit, her compassion, and her dedication to her work were qualities that made her stand out as a mother figure in the workplace. I am grateful to have had the opportunity to know and work alongside Trudie, and I will always cherish the memories of her kindness and support. She truly was a remarkable individual, and her presence in the office will be deeply missed.

Trudie Is not just a friend or mentor but a godly woman whose presence in my life has been a source of hope, guidance, and spiritual inspiration. Her unwavering faith, selfless love, and wise counsel have helped me navigate through some of the most challenging times in my life. I first met Trudie at a church event several years ago. From the moment I met her, I was struck by her grace, kindness, and genuine love for others. Trudie exuded a sense of peace and joy that was infectious, and I was drawn to her warmth and wisdom.

As I got to know Trudie better, I discovered that she was not just a woman of faith but a true influencer in the lives of those around her. Trudie had a gift for seeing the best in people and helping them tap into their potential. Whenever I felt lost or discouraged, Trudie was there to offer a listening ear, a word of encouragement, or a prayer to lift my spirits. Her presence in my life was a constant reminder of God's love and grace, and I found solace in her wisdom and faith.

One of the things that I admired most about Trudie was her unwavering faith in God. Trudie's faith was not just a set of beliefs but a way of life. She lived out her faith in all that she did, showing compassion, love, and grace to everyone she encountered. Trudie's faith was infectious, and her life was a testament to the power of God's love to transform lives. Trudie's faith was put to the test when she faced a series of challenges in her own life. She experienced loss, illness, and hardship, but through it all, she never wavered in her trust in God. Trudie's resilience and strength in the face of adversity inspired me to lean on my own faith in times of trouble. Her example taught me that no matter what storms may come, God is always there to guide us and strengthen us. Trudie's influence in my life was not just limited to times of trouble. She also inspired me to grow in my faith and deepen my relationship with God. Trudie shared her knowledge of scripture, her insights into prayer, and her experiences of God's faithfulness with me, helping me to see God in a new light.

Through Trudie's guidance, I was able to deepen my faith and trust in God's plan for my life. One of the things that I value most about my relationship with Trudie is her humility. Despite her wisdom, grace, and influence, Trudie always remained humble and grounded in her faith. She never sought recognition or praise for her actions but simply lived out her faith in a quiet and unassuming way. Trudie's humility taught me the importance of serving others selflessly and putting God's kingdom above my own desires. Trudie's impact on my life was profound and lasting. Her example of faith, love, and humility inspired me to live a life that reflects God's love and grace. Trudie's presence in my life was a constant source of hope, guidance, and spiritual inspiration, and I am grateful for her influence on my spiritual journey. Trudie Brand was not just a godly woman and influencer but a true beacon of light in a dark and troubled world. Her unwavering faith, selfless love, and wise counsel guided me through some of the most challenging times in my life. Trudie's example of faith, love, and humility inspired me to deepen my relationship with God and live out my faith in a way that honours Him. I am grateful for Trudie's presence in my life and the impact she has had on my spiritual journey. She will always hold a special place in my heart as a godly woman and influencer who has shown me the way to a deeper and more meaningful relationship with God.

In 2010, while I was working in the tasting room as a wine tasting host, I met a couple from the UK who came for a wine tasting. I conducted the tasting, and they bought a couple of excellent wines they loved: the Spice Route Malabar, a blend of Shiraz, Grenache, and Mourvèdre. They bought a couple of these bottles to take with them.

Two days later, I saw them walking in and they told me they had got engaged and they would love for me to be available when they got married. The groom was a South African, and they were going to get married in the Kruger National Park. This was like, wow, I just got invited to a wedding! They told me all expenses were paid, and all I needed was to book a flight. That, however, was a struggle for me. I had heard a lot of scary stories about flights, so I chose to book a bus. That was one of the best highlights of my life. We stayed in three camps: Berg-en-Dal Rest Camp, Biyamiti Bushveld Camp, and Lower Sabie. The wedding went well, but it was nerve-wracking for me as it took place in a Biyamiti Bushveld loop with armed rangers.

When my five days were over, I had to go back to work to process the payroll. With the payroll responsibility, my problems started. The farm had instated a savings system whereby farm workers would save money through the payroll. The new system came in as soon as I was appointed payroll clerk. Every week, people started pulling out their savings from the banks, and therefore, the payroll payment got bigger every week. I think at the time, the trust relationship between me and my colleagues was not yet established.

At the same time as the work challenges started getting to me, I started making friends, as I was also an excellent soccer player. After our soccer games, we would stay for drinks as a team. This habit grew upon us, a bunch of young players who just wanted to relax after a soccer game. I started having drinks even during the week while I was working on the wine farm; I had access to alcohol whenever I needed it, and that was extremely dangerous as we would meet at my place on Monday evenings as a team to discuss the previous Sunday's game over drinks. We did not see anything wrong with that, but the drinking habit was escalating. The drinking soon got out of control, but the discipline towards education was still intact.

On one baffling Saturday, while I was having drinks with my friends at one of our friends' homes, someone got into the yard from the back. I was standing in the street, having a cigarette. The drinking had quickly escalated to smoking, and this guy went inside; I went to attend to him, and we got into an intense argument. In no time, we fought he stabbed me between the collarbone and my back on the left side. I was rushed to Stellenbosch Hospital, and in the morning, when I woke up, the whole left side of my body had frozen up, and I had stitches. In no time, I recovered from this ordeal, and I then changed my ways.

Although my college studies were still going well, work pressure and money were starting to get to me. I had grown up without knowing anything about working with money, and suddenly, I was earning a couple of thousand rands. It was a great feeling, but dangerous. I continued to help my sister and sent money to my mom. In our Xhosa culture, if you are a firstborn and male, you have a responsibility to help your parent around the home together with your siblings. I did this with ease because I had no other responsibilities. My relationship with my childhood sweetheart was flourishing even though we were in a long-distance relationship, but we were fine.

In 2010, I noticed that my parent's relationship 'marriage' was taking another turn, and it was not looking good. We had been taught what a child's role in the family was, and we knew never to interfere in our elders' relationships. I kept quiet and kept on sending money to my mom as I was staying with my father at the time.

The Good Samaritan

During my time at Simonsvlei, I had the privilege of meeting Heila Brand, who worked closely with the workers and had a deep appreciation for my father's work ethic and commitment. When she discovered that I was his son, she took a keen interest in my future plans, particularly in terms of education. At that time, I had not given much thought to my future and had no concrete plans in place. However, Heila's inquiry about my aspirations planted a seed in my mind, which prompted me to consider the importance of education and its role in shaping my future.

When the opportunity for me to pursue further studies eventually arose, I found myself at a loss as to where to begin. It was then that I turned to Heila for guidance and support, as she had shown a genuine interest in my development. She graciously took the time to sit down and explain a plan of action, offering valuable insights and advice on how to navigate the complex world of education and career planning. Heila's mentorship and support proved to be invaluable, as her guidance helped me to chart a clear path forward and set achievable goals for myself. With her encouragement, I was able to take the necessary steps to further my education and pursue my aspirations with confidence. Her belief in my potential and her willingness to invest time and effort in my development was instrumental in shaping my future trajectory.

Through Heila's intervention, I not only gained a sense of direction and purpose but also learnt the importance of seeking guidance and support from mentors who genuinely cared about my well-being and success. Her impact on my life serves as a testament to the profound influence that a supportive mentor can have in shaping the course of one's future. Heila Brand's intervention in my life was a turning point that set me on a path towards personal and academic growth. Her genuine interest in my well-being and her willingness to offer guidance and support played a pivotal role in shaping my future aspirations. I am grateful for her mentorship and the positive impact she had on my life, and I am inspired to pay it forward by supporting others in their journey towards realising their full potential.

The White Brother I Never Had

In the realm of professional life, transitions and changes are inevitable. People may find themselves comfortable in their roles, enjoying responsibilities, and excelling in their positions. However, when a new colleague joins a team, it can sometimes lead to feelings of uncertainty and doubt. This was the case for me when Fairview employed Estienne Venter to work alongside me as a payroll administrator and human resources manager under the guidance of Andries Laker.

At first, the arrival of Estienne did not sit well with me. I could not help but feel a sense of apprehension and concern that perhaps my time at Fairview was ending. I was used to working independently and had established my own methods and ways of doing things. The prospect of having to adapt to a new working dynamic with Estienne seemed daunting and unsettling.

As we began working together, our relationship was somewhat rocky. I was resistant to change and did not take the time to learn Estienne's methods and approaches. Our interactions were strained, and there was a palpable tension between us. Misunderstandings and conflicts arose due to our differing work styles and communication preferences.

However, as time passed and we continued to collaborate on various projects and tasks, something unexpected happened. Despite our initial differences and challenges, Estienne and I gradually developed a mutual respect for each other's strengths and abilities. We began to complement each other's skills, with Estienne bringing a fresh perspective and innovative ideas to the table while I provided stability and experience. Through our shared experiences and shared goals, we realised that we could achieve more by working together rather than against each other.

Our collaboration evolved into a partnership built on trust, respect, and a shared commitment to excellence. We learnt to leverage each other's strengths and support each other in areas where we needed improvement. As our professional relationship blossomed, so did our personal connection. What started as a tentative working relationship transformed into a deep friendship based on mutual understanding, empathy, and shared values. Estienne became not only my business partner but also my confidant, adviser, and ally. We supported each other through challenges, celebrated successes together, and stood by each other through thick and thin.

Today, I can confidently say that Estienne is not just a colleague or a friend but someone I would take to war with me anytime. Our journey from initial scepticism and discord to a strong partnership and friendship is a testament to the power of collaboration, open-mindedness, and willingness to embrace change. Through our shared experiences, we have learnt the value of teamwork, communication, and mutual respect in achieving common goals and fostering meaningful relationships. While the arrival of Estienne initially stirred feelings of uncertainty and doubt within me, it ultimately led to a transformative journey of growth, learning, and friendship. Our ability to overcome differences, adapt to change, and embrace collaboration has not only strengthened our professional capabilities but also enriched our lives in ways we never imagined. I am grateful for the opportunity to work alongside Estienne and look forward to many more successful endeavours as business partners and best friends.

Marriage Life and Culture

In October 2012, I asked my childhood sweetheart for her hand in marriage, and she accepted, and we immediately started arranging the wedding. By this time, I was done with college. I asked my father to be one of the marriage negotiation delegates. In our Xhosa culture, lobola negotiations play a significant role in marriage traditions. Lobola, also known as 'the bride price', is a customary practice where the groom's family presents gifts or cattle to the bride's family as a gesture of respect and appreciation for their daughter. The negotiations are a formal process that involves both families coming together to discuss and agree upon the terms of the lobola.

During the negotiations, representatives from both families, usually elders or designated spokespeople, meet to discuss the number of cattle or other gifts to be exchanged. The negotiations can be a complex and delicate process, requiring diplomacy, respect, and patience from both sides. The lobola negotiations are not just about the exchange of gifts but also symbolise the coming together of two families and the establishment of a bond between them. It is a way to honour and acknowledge the bride's family for raising and nurturing their daughter, as well as to demonstrate the groom's commitment and ability to provide for his future wife. Lobola negotiations in Xhosa culture are a traditional practice that holds deep cultural and symbolic significance, emphasising the importance of family, respect, and unity in the union of marriage.

The marriage negotiations went well, and we set our date for 26 October 2013. We got married, and we moved back to Cape Town as we were both employed there. On Thursday, 7 November 2013, as we were ready to go, my mother asked that we say a prayer for the road. When we were done with the prayer, she held both our hands and gave us a gift of life.

She said, "In life, I do not have much. I am not a wealthy person, but please accept this gift from me as this is the only gift I can afford to give my children." She gave us a Bible, and she said that we would find all the answers to all the challenges we would encounter in the Bible, and we left.

In our Xhosa culture, it is a widespread practice for the bride to stay with her mother-in-law after marriage to learn about the family customs, traditions, and expectations. This period of cohabitation is known as "ukuHota" and serves as a time for the bride to integrate into her new family and community.

During her stay with her mother-in-law, the bride is expected to observe and participate in various household duties, rituals, and ceremonies. She learns about the family's history, values, and cultural practices, as well as how to navigate relationships within the extended family network. While the bride is busy learning from her in-laws, the groom is also learning from his father and observing the dynamics within his own family. This period of observation and learning is crucial for the groom as he navigates the transition from being a son to becoming a husband. He may observe how his father interacts with his mother, how decisions are made within the family, and how conflicts are resolved. These observations can provide valuable insights for the groom as he prepares to start his own family.

This period of transition is seen as an important rite of passage for the bride, allowing her to bond with her new family members, gain wisdom from her mother-in-law, and establish her role within the family structure. It also provides an opportunity for the bride to demonstrate her respect, humility, and willingness to adapt to her new surroundings.

The practice of the bride staying with her mother-in-law after marriage in Xhosa culture is a way to ensure the continuity of traditions, strengthen family ties, and facilitate the bride's integration into her new family and community. Unfortunately, we could not follow this practice as we needed to head back to work as we both were working.

When I got back to Cape Town, I had to relocate to Joe Slovo township in Milnerton, as my wife was employed in that area. Therefore, I had to commute every morning and every evening; sometimes, the trains would get stuck in the middle of nowhere, and I would arrive home extremely late. While we were trying to navigate through life and enjoy our marriage, we were blessed with a healthy baby, Luphiwe, Angela Kumatana. She was born on 31 August 2014, and we gave her, her middle name Angela, remembering our American friends, the Jones family.

When she started with daycare, things did not go well and we decided that my wife would stop working, which was not a straightforward decision as we needed the money, but the health of our baby was our priority. She then stopped working. Young marriage, while filled with love and excitement, can also present unique challenges for couples. We did not have life experiences to help us as individuals, and as a couple, we had to develop conflict-resolution skills and emotional maturity.

Without having had such experiences before, we struggled to navigate misunderstandings and disagreements healthily and constructively. Without a wealth of experiences to draw from, we found it challenging to make important decisions together, such as financial planning, career choices, or family planning.

This lack of life experience made it difficult for us to strike a balance between maintaining our individuality and building a strong partnership as a couple as we were in the process of figuring out what we wanted out of life. This led to uncertainty about our goals, values, and priorities, which in turn affected our ability to engage fully in the marriage. From 2013 to 2024, one of the most prominent struggles we faced as a couple was the ongoing battle to find a balance between tradition and religion. This issue permeated every aspect of our lives, from personal beliefs to family practices. Religion emerged as the biggest challenge we grappled with during this period.

The conflict between tradition and religion has been a longstanding one, rooted in fundamental differences between the two. While tradition is often seen as a set of customs or practices that have been passed down through generations, religion is a more formalised system of beliefs that governs the way people live their lives. In many cases, tradition and religion are intertwined, with religious beliefs forming the basis of cultural practices and customs. However, as a couple, the tension between these two forces can become more pronounced.

Over the past decade, we have seen this tension play out in a variety of ways; whether it was celebrating holidays and festivals or following specific dietary restrictions, tradition served as a way of connecting to the past and maintaining a sense of continuity in an ever-changing world. Religion emerged as a significant challenge during this period. As a couple, we turned to our faith for guidance and solace in the face of uncertainty, upheaval and religious beliefs. The clash of values, tradition and religion led to heated debates and deep discussions, which we could not seem to get to the end of.

As we struggled to find a balance between tradition and religion during this turbulent period, we were forced to confront some difficult truths about our marriage and ourselves. We grappled with the legacy which had imposed Western religious beliefs and practices on indigenous cultures and traditions. We confronted the inherent contradictions and hypocrisies of our own beliefs and practices as we struggled to reconcile the teachings of our faith with the realities of our daily lives.

In the end, the struggle to find a balance between tradition and religion was a deeply personal and collective one. It required us to confront our own biases and prejudices, to challenge the status quo, and to reimagine the way we understood and practised our faith. It forced us to listen to voices that had long been marginalised or silenced, to engage in difficult conversations with beliefs that differed from our own, and to make space for new and diverse perspectives. It called on us to embrace change and uncertainty, to question our assumptions and preconceptions, and to find common ground amidst our differences.

As we look to the future, the struggle to find a balance between tradition and religion will continue to shape our marriage in profound ways. We must be willing to confront the challenges and contradictions that arise from this tension, to engage in dialogue and reflection, and to seek out new ways of understanding and practising our faith. Only by embracing this complexity and diversity can we hope to forge a more just, inclusive, and compassionate marriage for future generations. In 2016, we decided to move to Kraaifontein, which was about twenty-six kilometres from my place of employment. In 2016, my colleague and I were approached by Charles Back, as we were the only two employees in the human resources department. He proposed that we might need to consider starting a human resourcing company and providing HR services to all his businesses. As part of the proposal, he wanted to start a business with us, and we agreed to take his offer. This was a bold decision because we were not guaranteed success. We had to work extra hard, and we needed an extra pair of hands. The HR industry is extremely competitive, and you need to know your story.

We started looking at a name for the business. We decided to name the business with the help of a public relations company. We named it Konnekt. We chose the name Konnekt because our job is to connect and build relationships between employees and their employers. We employed another payroll clerk as we saw that it was necessary. In 2017, we spoke to Charles about the possibility of buying him out, as this seemed to cause a conflict of interest because, currently, he had to sit on the boards of two companies. He accepted our proposal, and we bought him out by buying him a fitness bike to motivate him to stay healthy. After we bought him out, we then owned all the shares. We started sourcing outside businesses and building relationships. As I author this book, I am a forty-nine per cent shareholder of Konnekt PPC (People, Payroll, and Compliance), and the company has been in operation for seven years.

On 17 May 2017, we were blessed with another beautiful baby girl, Alulutho Alison Kumatana.

My Responsibilities As the Firstborn Son in My Family

In an African context, the duties of a firstborn male child can vary, as they are influenced by traditional practices and the specific cultural background of the family and community. Some common expectations were that the Xhosa people, who are one of the largest cultural groups in South Africa, have rich traditions and customs that shape the roles and expectations of people based on their age, gender, and position within the family structure.

The firstborn male is often expected to take on a leadership position within the family and community. This may involve making important decisions, providing guidance, and representing the family in various contexts. In Xhosa African culture, the role of the eldest son holds significant importance and carries various responsibilities within the family and the community.

The eldest son in Xhosa culture is typically accorded respect and authority within the family and community due to his age, experience, and position as a senior male member. He is often seen as a source of wisdom, guidance, and leadership, and his opinions and decisions usually carry significant weight in family matters.

When my father was still alive as the eldest son, I was phased into fulfilling the role of protector and provider for my family and ensuring the well-being, safety, and security of my loved ones. This involved taking on responsibilities such as providing financial support, offering emotional care, and safeguarding the family's interests.

As the eldest son, it became my responsibility to care for my ageing mother and other elderly relatives. Part of my responsibility included providing physical care, emotional support, and companionship to the elders, as well as ensuring that their needs were met and that their dignity was preserved in old age.

As time went by, I became a custodian and played a crucial role in preserving and passing down cultural traditions, values, and knowledge to younger generations. I became responsible for teaching cultural practices, rituals, and customs to my children and the grandchildren of the family, thereby ensuring the continuity of heritage and identity. I saw more responsibilities being added to my responsibilities, such as mediating and peace-making by resolving disputes and promoting harmony among family members. I saw the peace-making role as a key role as I was raised by peacemakers. My dad and mom loved peace and harmony.

Part of my responsibility as the oldest son is often seen as providing a link between past, present, and future generations, carrying the legacy of my ancestors and ensuring that their stories, values, and wisdom are passed down to future descendants. As the eldest son, I have to serve as a role model and mentor for the younger family members by offering guidance, support, and encouragement as they navigate life's challenges and transitions.

Growing up in a large household with three younger siblings, I quickly learnt the importance of setting a good example. My mother, a strong and wise woman, instilled in me the value of being a role model for my brother and sisters. Through her guidance and teachings, I have come to understand the impact that my actions and words have on those around me, especially on my younger siblings.

My mother always emphasised the responsibility that comes with being the eldest of four children. She taught me that my siblings look up to me and often model their behaviour after mine. As their older brother, it was my duty to lead by example and show them the right path to follow. This meant making good choices, treating others with kindness and respect, and always striving to do my best in everything I do. One of the most important lessons my mother taught me was the power of positive influence. She believed that the way I carried myself and the values I upheld would have a direct impact on my siblings. If I demonstrated honesty, integrity, and hard work, my siblings would be more likely to do the same. My mother made it clear that I had the potential to shape their beliefs, attitudes, and actions through my own behaviour.

My mother's teachings were not just words; she also led by example. She was a constant source of inspiration for me and my siblings, always displaying grace, strength, and compassion in everything she did. Whether it was caring for our family, excelling in her career, or helping others in need, my mother embodied the qualities she wanted us to emulate. She showed us that being a role model meant living out our values and beliefs every day, even when faced with challenges or adversity.

As I grew older, I began to appreciate the impact my mother's guidance had on me and my siblings. I realised that being a role model was not just about setting a good example. It was also about being a source of support, encouragement, and guidance for those looking up to me. My mother taught me that being a positive influence meant being there for my siblings when they needed me, listening to their concerns, and offering advice and guidance whenever possible. One of the most important ways I have been able to be a role model for my siblings is through my academic and personal achievements. My mother always stressed the importance of education and hard work, and she encouraged me to strive for excellence in everything I did. By excelling in school, pursuing my passions, and setting goals for myself, I have been able to show my siblings the value of determination, perseverance, and self-discipline.

In addition to my academic achievements, I have also tried to lead by example through my actions and behaviour. I try to treat others with kindness and respect, to be honest and trustworthy, and to always stand up for what I believe in. I try to be a positive influence on my siblings by demonstrating effective communication skills, problem-solving abilities, and leadership qualities.

Being a role model for my siblings has not always been easy. It has required patience, understanding, and a willingness to admit my own faults and shortcomings. There have been times when I have made mistakes, fallen short of my own expectations, or struggled to live up to the standards set by my mother. However, I have always strived to learn from my failures, grow from my experiences, and come back stronger and more determined to be the best brother and role model I can be. As I reflect on my upbringing and the lessons my mother taught me about being a role model for my siblings, I am grateful for the guidance and support she provided. Through her words and actions, my mother showed me the importance of setting a good example and being a source of inspiration and guidance for those who look up to me. I hope to continue to honour her teachings and to be a positive influence on my siblings, helping them to become the best version of themselves and to achieve their goals and dreams.

My mother taught me the value of being a role model for my siblings, of leading by example and showing them the right path to follow. Through her guidance and teachings, I have learnt the power of positive influence and the impact my actions and words have on those around me. I am grateful for the lessons my mother has taught me, and I will continue to strive to be the best brother and role model I can be for my siblings.

In 2020, my wife and I celebrated our seventh wedding anniversary full of difficulties. This year was particularly special to us as both of our children were available to join us in celebrating this milestone. However, there was a tinge of sadness as my mom, who has always been a pillar of support in our lives, could not attend the celebration due to the distance between us.

As we sat around the dinner table, reminiscing about the journey we had embarked on seven years ago, I could not help but feel a pang of longing for my mom's presence.

She had always been there for us, offering her love and guidance whenever we needed it. Her absence on such an important occasion was deeply felt by all of us. Despite the physical distance separating us, my mom was with us in spirit. I could almost hear her voice as we shared stories and laughter, her words of wisdom echoing in my mind. It was her unwavering support and belief in our love that had carried us through the tough times, and I knew that she was there with us, celebrating from afar.

As I looked around at my wife and my children, I felt grateful for the love and strength that our family had provided us with. Our marriage had weathered many storms, but it was the bond we shared with our loved ones that had kept us grounded and united. My mom may not have been able to attend our anniversary celebration physically. Still, her presence was felt in every moment as we celebrated the love and commitment that had brought us together.

During our joy and celebration, I could not help but reflect on the challenges we had faced during the past seven years. From financial struggles to health issues, we have been tested in ways we never could have imagined. But through it all, our love had remained steadfast, growing stronger with each passing day. As I look back on our journey, I realise that it was the love and support of our family that had carried us through the toughest times. My mom's absence on our anniversary was a reminder of the sacrifices she had made for us, and I felt a deep sense of gratitude for everything she had done for our family.

As the evening ended, I felt a sense of peace and contentment wash over me. Our marriage anniversary celebration had been a testament to the love and resilience that had sustained us through the years. Although my mom may not have been able to join us physically, her spirit was present in every moment, reminding us of the strength and love that we shared as a family.

Our marriage anniversary in 2020 was a bittersweet celebration marked by the absence of my mom. Though she may not have been able to attend in person, her love and support were felt throughout the evening, serving as a reminder of the importance of family in our lives. As we move forward into the future, we carry with us the lessons and love that we have learnt from our journey together, knowing that no matter the distance, our family will always be there to support and uplift us.

My Mother My Responsibility

Respect for one's mother is an integral part of a person's character and identity. Any man who lacks respect for his mother has lost touch with his true self and has strayed from the values that define him. A mother is a figure of love, sacrifice, and support in a person's life, and to dismiss or disregard her is to disregard one's own roots and upbringing. The relationship between a mother and her child is one of the most important and influential relationships in a person's life. From the moment a child is born, a mother is there to nurture, protect, and guide them. She is the first person to show them love and care and the one who teaches them the values and morals that will shape their character.

A mother sacrifices her own needs and desires for the sake of her children, and her love is unconditional and unwavering. To disrespect or disregard such a figure in one's life is to deny the very essence of who one is and where one comes from. Respect for one's mother is not just a matter of honouring a parental figure. It is also a reflection of one's own values and character. A man who disrespects his mother is showing a lack of gratitude for all that she has done for him and a disregard for the values and morals she has instilled in him. It is a sign of selfishness and immaturity, as it shows that he is unable to recognise and appreciate the sacrifices and love that his mother has given him. It also reflects a lack of empathy and compassion, as he is unable to put himself in his mother's shoes and understand the pain and hurt that his disrespect causes her. Moreover, disrespect towards one's mother can have far-reaching consequences, not just for the individual but for society.

A man who does not respect his mother is likely to have difficulty forming meaningful and healthy relationships with others, as he is unable to truly connect with and appreciate the value of those around him. He may struggle in his personal and professional life, as his lack of respect for his mother reflects a lack of respect for authority and societal norms. It may also lead to a cycle of disrespect and abuse towards others, as he has not learnt to value and honour the relationships in his life.

On the other hand, a man who respects and honours his mother is a man who is in touch with his true self and his values. He recognises the love, sacrifice, and support that his mother has given him, and he is grateful for it. He understands the importance of family and relationships, and he values the lessons and morals that his mother has taught him. He is empathetic, compassionate, and respectful towards others, as he has learnt the importance of treating others with kindness and dignity.

He is grounded in his identity and values and able to navigate the challenges and struggles of life with grace and humility. Any man who has no respect for his mother has lost his way and his true self. Respect for one's mother reflects one's character, values, and identity. It is a recognition of the love, sacrifice, and support that she has given to the family and a tribute to the lessons and morals that she has taught. Disrespect towards one's mother is a sign of immaturity, selfishness, and a lack of empathy and compassion. It can have far-reaching consequences, not just for the individual but for society.

On the other hand, a man who respects and honours his mother is a man who is in touch with his true self and his values and who can flourish and thrive in all aspects of his life. Respect for one's mother is not just a duty, but it reflects one's character and identity and is a testament to the values and morals that define who we are.

As the firstborn son in my family, I have always been aware of the expectations placed upon me to take care of my mother, especially in situations where my father is unable to fulfil his duties. This responsibility is deeply ingrained in our cultural beliefs and traditions, and I have taken it upon myself to honour this duty to the best of my abilities. My role as the firstborn son is often seen as one of significant importance. I believe that I carry the burden of taking care of my parents as they age, ensuring their well-being and providing for their needs. This responsibility is passed down from generation to generation and is considered a vital part of family life.

When my father fell ill and was unable to work, the responsibility of caring for my mother fell solely on my shoulders. As the eldest son, it was expected that I would step up and take on this role without hesitation. While it was a daunting task to assume such a level of responsibility at a youthful age, I knew that it was my duty to care for my mother in her time of need.

Taking care of my mother meant providing for her financial needs, ensuring she had access to proper healthcare, and taking care of the household chores. It also meant being there for her emotionally, offering support and comfort during challenging times.

As her son, I made it my mission to do everything in my power to make sure she was well taken care of and felt loved and supported. In African culture, the bond between a mother and her eldest son is a special one. It is believed that the firstborn son carries the spirit of his ancestors and plays a crucial role in upholding the family's values and traditions. This bond between a mother and her son is one of mutual respect and love, and it is through this connection that the responsibility of care is passed down from generation to generation.

As the firstborn son, it was not only my duty to care for my mother but also to honour and respect her. I understood the sacrifices she had made for our family, and I was determined to repay her kindness and love by being there for her when she needed me the most. I knew that my actions would not only reflect on myself, but also on my family and the ancestors who came before me.

Despite the challenges that came with taking on the responsibility of caring for my mother, I considered it a privilege to be able to repay her love and devotion in this way. I knew that by fulfilling my duties as the eldest son, I was upholding the traditions and values of my family and community. I also understood that my actions would set an example for my siblings and future generations to follow.

The responsibility of caring for a mother in African culture is a sacred duty that falls upon the shoulders of the eldest son. As the firstborn son in my family, I have embraced this responsibility with pride and dedication, knowing that I must care for my mother in her time of need. By honouring this duty, I am not only upholding the traditions and values of my family, but I am also demonstrating my love and respect for my mother. The bond between a mother and her eldest son is a special one, rooted in love, respect, and mutual understanding.

Through this bond, the responsibility of care is passed down from generation to generation, ensuring that the legacy of family and tradition lives on. With my dad having passed on, due to my culture and upbringing, it became an expectation and later a reality to care for my mom and siblings and the extended family members from both my parent's sides without favouring some more than others. This expectation is rooted in cultural norms, values, and the concept of filial piety, which emphasises the importance of honouring and supporting one's parents and elders.

One of the primary financial responsibilities of an elderly son is to provide financial support for his ageing parents. This support may include covering their living expenses, medical bills, and other essential needs to ensure their well-being and comfort in their old age. Part of my financial responsibilities as the eldest son is that I was often expected to contribute financially to the overall household expenses, including food, shelter, utilities, and other necessities. This contribution helps to alleviate the financial burden on the family and ensures that everyone's needs are met.

Raising Our Two Beautiful Daughters

When my daughters were younger, changing their nappies was a part of my daily routine that I will never forget. It was a task that required patience, care, and love, but it was also a time that allowed me to bond with my daughters uniquely.

As a father, I took considerable pride in being able to take care of my daughters in this way and provide them with the comfort and cleanliness they needed. I remember the first time I changed my daughters' nappies like it was yesterday. It was a daunting task at first, as I had never done it before, and I was worried about making a mistake.

However, with the guidance of my wife and some helpful tips from friends and family, I quickly got the hang of it. I learnt how to clean them thoroughly and dispose of the nappy, how to apply the cream to prevent rashes, and how to fasten the new nappy in place securely.

Despite the initial challenges, changing my daughters' nappies soon became a familiar and almost meditative experience for me. It was a time when I could focus solely on my daughters' needs and show them my love and care in a very tangible way. I would talk to them softly, sing songs, and make silly faces to keep them entertained while I changed them. This time spent together created a special bond between us that I will always cherish.

As my daughters grew older, changing their nappies became less of a task and more of a routine. They would wriggle and squirm as I tried to fasten the new nappy in place, giggling and cooing all the while. I would playfully tickle them and make funny noises to keep them calm and happy during the process. It became a game for them, a time of laughter and joy that they looked forward to every day. I also discovered that changing my daughters' nappies was an opportunity to observe their development and growth.

I would marvel at how quickly they were growing, how their little bodies were changing and developing right before my eyes. It was a constant reminder of the passage of time and the precious moments I had with them as they were still small and dependent on me for everything. There were, of course, moments of frustration and exhaustion.

There were times when my daughters would refuse to lie still or would have a particularly messy diaper that seemed impossible to clean up. But even in those moments, I reminded myself of the love and care I had for my daughters and how important it was to provide them with a clean and comfortable environment.

As my daughters grew older and eventually outgrew their nappies, I found myself reminiscing about those early days of fatherhood. Changing their nappies had become a routine that I had come to cherish, a time when I could bond with my daughters. It was a simple act of love and care that had a profound impact on our relationship and my role as a father. Today, as I look back on those days of changing my daughters' nappies, I am grateful for the experience and the memories it created. It was a time of growth, learning, and love that shaped me as a father and deepened my connection with my daughters. I will always treasure those moments and the special bond that was formed during those simple yet profound acts of care and love.

In many African cultures, it is believed that a woman's primary responsibility is to care for her children. This includes putting a child on her back and wrapping them in a towel, a practice that has been passed down through generations. This tradition is not just about practicality but also about building a strong bond between mother and child from an early age. I vividly remember the first time I put my child on my back and wrapped them in a towel. It was a moment of pure joy and love as I felt their tiny body against mine, knowing that they were safe and secure. From that moment on, I made a conscious decision to always carry my children in this way, regardless of who was watching or what others might say. It was a connection that went beyond just physical closeness - it was a bond of trust and love that would last a lifetime.

As my children grew older, they became used to being carried on my back. It became a routine part of our daily lives, whether we were going to the market, visiting family, or simply going for a walk. They would wrap their tiny arms around me, feeling the warmth of my body and the comfort of being close to their parents. It was a simple act, but it spoke volumes about the deep connection we shared. I never once considered what others might think of this practice. To me, it was a natural and instinctive way of caring for my children. I was not concerned with whether people would judge me for carrying my child in this way or if it were seen as unconventional. What mattered most to me was the bond that I was building with my children, the sense of security and comfort that they felt when held close to me.

As my children grew older, they started to walk, but even then, they would often come back to me, seeking the familiar comfort of being carried on my back. It was a ritual that we both cherished, a moment of closeness and connection in a busy world. Looking back now, I realise the importance of building such a strong relationship with my children from an early age. It laid the foundation for a deep and lasting bond that has only grown stronger over the years. My children still remember those moments of being carried on my back, the feeling of safety and love that enveloped them when they were close to me.

In African culture, the practice of carrying a child on one's back is not just about physical closeness - it is a symbol of love, care, and protection. It is a way for a mother to show her child that they are always there for them, no matter what. It is a tradition that has been passed down through generations, a reminder of the strong bonds that connect us to our children and each other. I am proud to have carried on this tradition with my children and to have built a relationship based on love, trust, and closeness. As they continue to grow and flourish, I know that the memories of being carried on my back will always be with them, a reminder of the strong bond that we share. It is a tradition that I will continue to cherish, a practice that speaks volumes about the beauty and depth of African culture.

As my children grew older, our family dynamics began to change. Our busy schedules, extracurricular activities, and work responsibilities often left us with little time to bond and connect. However, I wanted to make sure that we still had special moments together, so I started a tradition where I would take my children out for ice cream. It started as a simple idea – a treat to help us unwind and spend quality time together. However, as we continued this tradition, it became so much more than just ice cream. It became a time for us to catch up, share stories, and laugh together. There was something magical about sitting in the ice cream shop, with each of us enjoying our favourite flavours and talking about our day. It was in these moments that we truly connected and formed a bond that extended beyond just being a family. I cherished these outings with my children, as they allowed me to see them in a different light. I could see them growing and maturing right before my eyes, and our conversations became more meaningful and insightful.

As they grew older, our ice cream outings became less frequent, but the memories we created during those times will stay with me forever. It was during these simple moments that I realised how important it is to be available for the ones we love and to cherish the moments we have together. Taking my children out for ice cream may have started as a simple tradition, but it became a significant part of our family's story. It reminded us of the importance of spending time together and creating memories that would last a lifetime. In every home, there are traditions that we hold near and dear to our hearts. These traditions help to bring families closer together and create lasting memories that we can cherish for years to come. In my family, one of our most cherished traditions is celebrating birthdays at our favourite restaurant, Spur.

Spur is a popular family-friendly restaurant known for its delicious food and welcoming atmosphere. It is a place where families can come together to enjoy a meal and create lasting memories. For as long as I can remember, my family has celebrated birthdays at Spur. It has become a tradition that we all look forward to each year.

On the day of our birthdays, we all gather as a family to celebrate. We exchange gifts, share laughter, and reminisce about past birthdays, and without fail, we always end up at Spur for our birthday meal. It has become a tradition that we all love and cherish. For us, going to Spur is more than just a meal. It is a time to come together as a family and celebrate the life of the person whose birthday it is. We enjoy the delicious food, the friendly staff, and the warm atmosphere that Spur provides. It is a tradition that has brought us closer together as a family and has created lasting memories that we will always hold dear.

One of the reasons why we love celebrating birthdays at Spur is because of the special treatment we receive as birthday guests. The staff at Spur always goes beyond the limit to make the birthday person feel special. From singing happy birthday to providing a complimentary dessert, the staff at Spur never fails to make the birthday celebration extra special. Another reason we love going to Spur for birthdays is because of the delicious food. Spur offers a wide variety of menu options that cater to everyone's taste. Whether you are in the mood for a juicy burger, a sizzling steak, or a refreshing salad, Spur has something for everyone. And let us not forget about their famous bottomless soda fountain and delectable desserts.

It is no wonder why Spur is our go-to restaurant for birthday celebrations. But more than the food and the special treatment, celebrating birthdays at Spur is about creating memories with the ones we love. It is about coming together as a family to celebrate the life of a loved one and create lasting memories that we will always hold dear. The laughter, the joy, and the love that fills the air during our birthday celebrations at Spur are priceless and irreplaceable. Celebrating birthdays at Spur has become a tradition that we all cherish in our homes. It is a time for us to come together as a family, enjoy delicious food, and create lasting memories with the ones we love. The special treatment we receive as birthday guests, the delicious food, and the warm atmosphere of Spur make it the perfect place to celebrate birthdays. It is a tradition that we will continue to uphold for years to come, creating memories that will last a lifetime.

Marriage is a sacred union between two individuals, joined together in love, commitment, and companionship. But for my wife and I, our marriage is not only about the love we have for each other – it is also about the solid foundation of faith that we have built our relationship upon. From the beginning of our marriage, we both agreed on the importance of God in our lives, our marriage, and in raising our two beautiful daughters in the name of the Lord.

As a Christian couple, we understand the significance of having God at the centre of our marriage. We believe that God has brought us together for a purpose, and that purpose is to glorify Him in all that we do. By placing our faith in God, we have found strength, guidance, and wisdom to navigate the challenges and joys of married life. Through prayer, scripture reading, and attending church regularly, we have cultivated a deep relationship with God that has sustained us through the difficulties of life.

One of the key aspects of our marriage that is deeply rooted in our faith is communication. We believe that open and honest communication is essential for a strong and healthy marriage. By following the example of Jesus Christ and practising love, patience, and forgiveness in our interactions with each other, we have been able to resolve conflicts and misunderstandings peacefully and lovingly. We are always available to pray together, seek God's guidance, and lift each other in prayer when we face challenges. Raising our two daughters in the name of the Lord is a responsibility that we take very seriously.

We believe that it is our duty as parents to teach our children about God's love, grace, and mercy. We strive to be positive role models for our daughters, showing them the importance of faith, love, and compassion in all that we do. We read Bible stories to them, pray together as a family, and take them to church regularly so they can develop a solid foundation of faith in their lives.

Our faith has also played a significant role in shaping our parenting style. We strive to raise our daughters with Christian values such as kindness, honesty, and respect for others. We teach them to love their neighbours as themselves, to forgive others as God has forgiven them, and to always trust in God's plan for their lives.

By instilling these values in our daughters, we hope to raise them to be strong, compassionate, and God-fearing individuals who will make a positive impact on the world.

In times of difficulty and uncertainty, we turn to God for strength and comfort. We believe that God is always with us, guiding us through life's challenges and providing us with the strength to persevere. Through prayer and faith, we have experienced God's grace and mercy in our lives, and we know that He is always there to support us in times of need. The presence of God has blessed our marriage, and we are grateful for the love, grace, and guidance that He has provided us with.

By placing our faith in God, we have built a foundation of love, trust, and commitment that has strengthened our marriage and brought us closer together as a couple. We know that with God at the centre of our marriage, we can overcome any challenge that comes our way and continue to grow in love and faith together.

The importance of God in our marriage and in raising our two daughters cannot be overstated. Our faith has provided us with the strength, guidance, and wisdom to navigate the joys and challenges of married life and to raise our daughters with love, compassion, and Christian values.

By placing our trust in God, we have built a solid foundation for our marriage and family, and we know that with His grace and mercy, we can overcome any obstacle that comes our way. We are eternally grateful for the love and blessings that God has bestowed upon us, and we will continue to place our faith in Him as we journey through life together as a family.

My Role As a Present Father to My Daughters

As a father of two young girls, I take my role very seriously. Being a present father means being actively involved in every aspect of my daughters' lives, from their physical and emotional well-being to their education and personal development. I strive to create a strong bond with my daughters and be a positive influence in their lives.

One of the most important ways I fulfil my role as a present father is through spending quality time with my daughters. Whether it is playing at the park, reading bedtime stories, or just having a heart-to-heart conversation, I make sure to take time out of my busy schedule to be present and engage with my girls. This quality time together helps to build a sturdy foundation of trust and love between us.

I also make it a priority to be involved in my daughters' education. I attend parent-teacher conferences, help with homework, and take an active interest in their academic progress. A good education is essential for my daughters' future success, and I want to support them in any way I can to help them reach their full potential. In addition to their education, I also strive to instil important values and life skills in my daughters. I teach them about kindness, empathy, and respect for others, and I model these behaviours in my own interactions with them and with others. I believe that by setting a positive example, I can help my daughters grow into kind, compassionate individuals who contribute positively to their communities.

As a present father, I also prioritise my daughters' physical health and well-being. I encourage them to participate in sports and other physical activities, and I make sure they eat nutritious meals and get plenty of rest. I want my daughters to grow up healthy and strong, and I do my best to support them in making healthy choices for themselves. Being a present father also means being there for my daughters during challenging times. I listen to their problems and concerns, offer my guidance and support, and help them navigate through life's challenges.

I want my daughters to know that they can always come to me with any issue, big or small and that I will do everything in my power to help them through it. Overall, my role as a present father in my daughters' lives is one of love, support, and guidance. I strive to be a positive role model for my daughters, to provide them with the tools they need to succeed in life and to be a constant source of love and support for them. I am committed to being present and actively involved in my daughters' lives, and this is the most significant role I will ever have.

I make sure that they understand what being a father is, that I have to say No to certain things, and that I must maintain discipline around the house. I am also teaching them that in life, nothing is for free. If you want something, there is always a price that you must pay for it. In life, nothing will be handed to you on a silver platter for you to enjoy. My daughters must work hard to achieve whatever it is they want in life. As a present father, I do take on certain chores in the house that I am also involved in, like doing dishes and mopping the floor or picking up papers around the yard.

Preserving Cultural Traditions

The role of the firstborn son in preserving the culture and traditions of his family is crucial to many societies, especially in traditional and indigenous communities where cultural heritage holds significant value. As a custodian of ancestral knowledge, values, and practices, the eldest son plays a key role in passing down traditions to future generations and ensuring the continuity of cultural identity. The elderly son serves as a storyteller and keeper of oral history, recounting tales, myths, legends, and family narratives that convey cultural values, beliefs, and experiences. Through storytelling, he transmits knowledge and wisdom to younger family members, thereby preserving the collective memory of the family and community.

My role as the eldest son is to impart cultural practices, rituals, ceremonies, and customs to younger generations by teaching them how to perform traditional dances, songs, prayers, and other rituals that are integral to the family's cultural heritage. By participating in these activities, I am teaching the younger family members to learn to appreciate and respect their cultural roots. Part of my role as an elderly son is to oversee and participate in family rituals and ceremonies that mark important life events such as births, weddings, funerals, and other milestones. These rituals have deep cultural significance and serve to strengthen family bonds, honour ancestors, and reaffirm cultural values. It also forms part of my responsibility to provide guidance and advice on cultural etiquette, values, and norms to younger family members, thereby helping them to navigate social interactions, ceremonies, and community engagements with respect and sensitivity to cultural traditions.

Appreciation Phase

I am grateful for the opportunities provided to me. They were not provided because I deserved it. They were provided because of God's grace. Education has long been recognised as a powerful tool for personal growth, social mobility, and economic empowerment.

For many parents. In the past, the desire to provide better education opportunities for their children was driven by a deep-seated aspiration to break down barriers, create opportunities, and pave the way for a brighter future.

In this book, I am exploring the transformative journey of an uneducated parent who, through the opportunities of study and employment, has been able to afford better education for their children, thus setting the stage for a generational shift towards success and fulfilment.

As I navigate this transformative journey, I am not only shaping the future of my own family but also contributing to the larger narrative of empowerment and progress within our workplace environment and communities. The ripple effects of the actions of the people who extend their hand beyond the present moment lay the groundwork for a legacy of education, aspiration, and through their actions.

Those types of people not only provided better education and employment opportunities to me but also inspired hope, resilience, and possibility in others who were on a similar journey.

By seizing the opportunities presented to me and prioritising education as a means for change, I created a pathway towards a brighter future filled with possibilities and promise. My story serves as a reminder of the profound impact that education can have in shaping lives, breaking barriers, and unlocking the potential for success.

I would like to express my deepest gratitude to all those who took the time to read my book. Your support and interest mean the world to me, and I am incredibly grateful for your involvement in this literary journey. Authoring this book was never an easy task. It required countless hours of dedication, passion, and commitment to bring the story to life. However, knowing that there are readers out there eager to explore and immerse themselves in the world I created is truly inspiring. As a story narrator, my greatest joy comes from connecting with readers as they enjoy and benefit from this wonderful art form.

Whether you followed my characters, resonated with the themes, or simply enjoyed the narrative, I hope that my life journey provided you with an enjoyable and thought-provoking experience. Your engagement as a reader plays an integral role in shaping the future of my writing. I am eternally grateful for your support, which not only motivates me to keep writing but also strengthens my belief in the power of storytelling.

I want to extend a heartfelt thank you to every reader who has picked up a copy of this book and delved into its pages. Your presence throughout this journey has been invaluable, and I am honoured to have had the opportunity to share my life journey with you.

Dear Angela and Travis Jones,

I wanted to take a moment to express my deepest gratitude for your incredible generosity and kindness in paying for my college tuition. Your selfless act has not only lifted a tremendous financial burden off my shoulders but has also opened doors of opportunity that I never thought possible. Words cannot adequately convey the immense gratitude and appreciation I feel towards both of you. Your belief in my potential and your willingness to invest in my education have touched my heart in ways I cannot fully express.

Your support has not only made my dreams of higher education a reality but has also given me the chance to pursue my passions and strive for a brighter future. Your act of kindness not only impacted my life but will also have a ripple effect on my family and future generations. Your generosity has inspired me to work harder, dream bigger, and make a positive difference in the world. I am determined to make the most of this incredible opportunity you provided me with and to honour your investment in my education. Please know that your kindness will never be forgotten. I promise to make the most of this opportunity and to pay it forward in any way I can. Your belief in me has given me the confidence to pursue my goals with renewed determination and to strive for excellence in all that I do. I am proud to say that I have transformed personally and academically thanks to your support.

Once again, thank you sincerely for your incredible generosity and support. I am forever grateful for your kindness and will always cherish the impact you have had on my life.

Dear Charles Back,

Not only have you helped me financially, but you have also gone beyond the limit in empowering me to reach my fullest potential. The educational resources and opportunities Fairview offered opened doors for me that I never thought were possible. Through your guidance and support, I have grown both personally and professionally, gaining valuable experiences that will continue to shape my life for years to come. In addition to your generosity, I am incredibly grateful for the employment opportunities you have provided. The opportunities Fairview extended to me have not only allowed me to gain vital work experience but they gave me a chance to develop key skills and build a promising career. I am truly blessed to be part of such a supportive and nurturing workplace.

Once again, I cannot express enough how thankful I am for your unwavering support. Fairview's commitment to assisting individuals like me in pursuing higher education and achieving their goals is truly commendable. I feel incredibly fortunate to be a recipient of your generosity and dedication. Thank you once again, Charles Back, for everything you have done for me. Your support will forever hold a special place in my heart. I am committed to upholding the values and mission of Fairview in my future endeavours, ensuring that your efforts and contributions are continued and appreciated.

Dear Heila Brand,

I wanted to take a moment to express my heartfelt gratitude for the support you have provided me. Your unwavering belief in me and your constant encouragement has been instrumental in my personal and professional growth. Your support has come in many forms - whether it be lending a listening ear, offering guidance and advice, or simply being there for me during challenging times. Your presence in my life has been a source of strength and inspiration, and I am profoundly grateful for your unwavering support. Your belief in my abilities has given me the confidence to pursue my dreams and overcome any obstacles that come my way. Your emotional support has pushed me to step outside my comfort zone and strive for excellence in all that I do. Your unwavering support has been a constant reminder that I am not alone on this journey, and for that, I am eternally grateful.

I want you to know that your support has made a significant impact on my life. Your kindness and generosity have not gone unnoticed, and I am truly blessed to have you in my corner. Your belief in me has given me the strength to persevere and has inspired me to reach for the stars.

Thank you, Heila, for being a pillar of support in my life. Your kindness, encouragement, and unwavering belief in me have made a world of difference. I am forever grateful for your presence and the positive impact you have had on my life.

With deepest gratitude.

To my Wife and Kids!

Nolusindiso Portia Kumatana, Kids, and all those who have had a positive impact on my life.

I wanted to take a moment to express my heartfelt gratitude and appreciation for the unwavering support and love you have shown me. Your presence in my life has been a constant source of strength and inspiration, and I am truly blessed to have you by my side.

To my dear wife, thank you for being my rock and my partner in every aspect of life. Your unwavering love, understanding, and patience have been my guiding light through the difficulties. Your support has given me the courage to chase my dreams and overcome any obstacles that come my way. I am forever grateful for your presence in my life.

To my incredible kids, you are my pride and joy. Your laughter, innocence, and unconditional love have brought immense happiness into my life. Your unwavering belief in me has pushed me to be the best version of myself. Watching you grow and thrive fills my heart with immense joy and gratitude. Thank you for being my greatest motivation.

To all those who have had a positive impact on my life, whether it be friends, mentors, or family members, thank you for your guidance, encouragement, and belief in me. Your presence has shaped me into the person I am today, and I am forever grateful for the lessons and experiences we have shared.

In times of triumph and moments of struggle, your unwavering support has been the driving force behind my success. Your belief in me has given me the confidence to pursue my dreams and overcome any challenges that come my way. I am truly blessed to have such an incredible support system.

To my family, thank you for the gift of your presence, your love, and your unwavering support. You have enriched my life beyond measure, and I am forever grateful for the privilege of walking this journey with each one of you. Let us continue to cherish, nurture, and celebrate the ties that bind us, knowing that our family's legacy will endure, etched in the hearts and souls of all whom our love has touched.

Thank you sincerely for being there for me and for being an integral part of my journey. Your love, support, and impact on my life are immeasurable, and I am forever grateful.

With deepest gratitude.

Acknowledging the Role of a Book Cover Designer

Book designers play a crucial role in bringing the words of an author to life. They are responsible for creating visually appealing layouts, selecting fonts, designing covers, and ensuring that the overall aesthetic of the book aligns with its content. A skilled book designer like Rozel Archer can enhance the reading experience and capture the essence of the story through thoughtful design choices.

Rozel Archer's design work has added another layer of depth and beauty to the books. From the striking cover designs that entice readers to pick up the books to the meticulous interior layouts that guide the reader through the stories, Rozel Archer's touch is evident in every aspect of the series.

It is important to recognise and appreciate the efforts of individuals like Rozel Archer, whose creativity and talent often go unnoticed behind the scenes. The impact of a book designer on the overall success of a book cannot be overstated, and their contribution deserves to be celebrated. Therefore, on behalf of all the readers who have been enchanted by the 'All the Footsteps' series, we extend our heartfelt thanks to Rozel Archer for their exceptional work.

Rozel Archer's role as the book designer of the 'All the Footsteps' series has been instrumental in shaping the visual identity of the books and enhancing the reading experience for countless readers. Rozel's talent, dedication, and creative vision have brought the world of the series to life in a way that words alone cannot express.

As we turn the pages of these books and immerse ourselves in their stories, let us not forget to say thank you to Rozel Archer for her invaluable contribution to the world of literature.

………………………………. The Journey Continues…………………

www.ingramcontent.com/pod-product-compliance
Lightning Source LLC
Chambersburg PA
CBHW072007290426
44109CB00018B/2163